THE AUSTRALIAN

Women's Weekly
new barbecues

PREPARATION

Barbecues have char-grills and/or solid plates; determine what's needed on the day and adjust the barbie to suit your needs before you heat it (on the highest setting with the hood closed). If the barbie has been oiled after the last use, there should be no need to oil the cooking surface; just apply oil lightly to the food to be cooked.

COOKING

Start by buying good quality tender cuts of meat – fast cooking on the barbie gives the best results. All food should be at room temperature before barbecuing. Once cooked, meat should be rested, covered loosely with foil on a warm plate. This allows the juices to settle, resulting in more tender meat.

Indirect cooking is efficient and gives good results. Place the food on the preheated barbie with a little space between each piece of food, close the hood, turn the heat off directly under the food and adjust the burner/s to the side/s of the food to a medium setting. Cook the food until it's half done, turn it over (only turn once), close the hood and continue cooking until the food is done. Barbecuing time depends on what is being cooked and how rare, or well-done, you like it cooked, particularly when it comes to beef, lamb and pork. Some *small, hooded barbecues* have just one wrap-around burner; in this case, add the food to the preheated barbie, close the hood and reduce the heat under the food to low/medium.

Direct cooking is done with the hood open (if there is a hood) and the food is cooked directly over the burners. Adjust the heat according to the food being cooked.

A lot of barbecues have *wok burners:* heat the wok over the highest heat, oil the wok, then stir-fry the food in small batches over a high heat until it's done.

salads & vegetables

contents

The oven temperatures in this book are for conventional ovens; if you have a fan-forced oven, decrease the temperature by 10-20 degrees.

barbecue essentials

THE BARBECUE

It doesn't really matter what kind of barbecue or what type of fuel is used to cook food, it's all about heat control and timing, but, these days, most at-home barbies are gas-fuelled. The rules for using these are simple: keep them clean and heat them well before beginning to cook – all the finer points that apply to individual models can be found in the instruction manual of each barbecue type.

Keep a spare full gas bottle just in case the gas runs out mid-barbecue. Buy and install a gas fuse gadget from hardware or barbecue shops; these gadgets act like an electrical circuit breaker for the gas bottle being used. As well as making the use of gas bottles safer, it indicates how much gas is left in the bottle.

Hooded barbecues are really large outdoor ovens in disguise. With practice, most things you can cook in a normal kitchen oven can be cooked in a barbie with a hood. In the absence of a hood, try using a large high lid – those used for woks are excellent, or an unloved deep baking dish – to cover and enclose the food. The hood and lid method shortens the cooking time and helps keep the food moist.

CLEANING

After the cooking has finished, close the hood on the barbie, turn the setting to the highest possible heat, and let any food residue burn off – this will take about 10 minutes. When the barbie has cooled down, use a scraper to get rid of any large lumps of charcoal or food, then take to all of the exposed surfaces inside the barbie with a wire brush that's been dipped often into a bucket of cold water – detergent isn't necessary. Spray the interior of the barbie with an oil spray – the best type is one specifically designed for this job. This simple cleaning and oiling should maintain the barbecue for many years. If the barbecue is used a lot, a thorough annual clean-up will keep it in tip-top condition.

beetroot, pecan and goat's cheese salad

1kg (2 pounds) baby beetroot (beets), trimmed
1 small kumara (orange sweet potato) (250g),
  sliced thinly
1 tablespoon walnut or olive oil
1 tablespoon red wine vinegar
90g (3 ounces) spinach leaves
½ cup (60g) pecans, roasted, chopped coarsely
125g (4 ounces) goat's cheese, crumbled
⅓ cup fresh flat-leaf parsley leaves

1 Wrap each beetroot in foil; cook on heated barbecue (or grill or grill pan) about 35 minutes or until tender. Cool slightly, then peel and cut in half.
2 Meanwhile, cook kumara, in batches, on heated oiled barbecue until tender.
3 To make dressing, combine oil and vinegar in screw-top jar; shake well, season to taste.
4 Combine spinach, nuts, beetroot and kumara in bowl; top with cheese and parsley, then drizzle with dressing.

prep + cook time 45 minutes **serves** 4
nutritional count per serving 20.8g total fat
(4.6g saturated fat); 1492kJ (357 cal);
27.5g carbohydrate; 11.4g protein; 9.6g fibre

rosemary vegetable skewers

Boil, steam or microwave 16 baby new potatoes and 625g (1¼ pounds) coarsely chopped pumpkin, separately, until almost tender; drain. Meanwhile, finely grate 2 teaspoons of rind from 1 lemon; squeeze lemon, reserve 2 tablespoons juice. Trim and reserve leaves from bottom two-thirds of 8 x 15cm (6 inch) fresh rosemary sprigs; sharpen trimmed ends to a point. Finely chop 2 teaspoons of reserved leaves. Combine potato, pumpkin and 1 halved, thickly sliced large zucchini with the rind, juice, chopped rosemary and 2 crushed garlic cloves in large bowl; season. Thread vegetables onto rosemary skewers; cook skewers on heated oiled barbecue (or grill or grill pan), basting occasionally with reserved juice, about 10 minutes or until vegetables are tender.

prep + cook time 40 minutes **makes** 8
nutritional count per skewer 0.7g total fat (0.3g saturated fat); 397kJ (95 cal); 16.1g carbohydrate; 3.9g protein; 3g fibre

mexican vegetable skewers

Thickly slice 2 trimmed corn cobs. Coarsely chop 1 medium green capsicum (bell pepper). Cut 1 small red onion into 8 wedges. Combine corn, capsicum, onion and 250g (8 ounces) cherry truss tomatoes with 35g (1 ounce) packet taco seasoning and 2 tablespoons bottled chunky tomato salsa in large bowl; season. Thread vegetables onto 8 metal skewers; cook skewers on heated oiled barbecue (or grill or grill pan) about 15 minutes. Serve skewers with extra 1⅓ cups bottled chunky tomato salsa.

prep + cook time 35 minutes **makes** 8
nutritional count per skewer 9g total fat (0.3g saturated fat); 978kJ (234 cal); 37g carbohydrate; 9.1g protein; 10.6g fibre

serving suggestion Sour cream and tortillas.

note We used metal skewers to pierce through the hard core of the corn slices.

honey, soy and sesame eggplant skewers

Peel and coarsely chop 1 large eggplant; place, in single layer, in large bamboo steamer. Place steamer over large pan of simmering water; steam eggplant about 5 minutes or until tender. Thread eggplant onto 8 bamboo skewers. Whisk ¼ cup kecap manis, 1 tablespoon honey and 1 teaspoon sesame oil in small bowl until combined. Brush honey mixture over skewers; cook skewers on heated oiled barbecue (or grill or grill pan), basting occasionally with remaining honey mixture, about 5 minutes, or until browned. Serve skewers sprinkled with 2 teaspoons roasted sesame seeds.

prep + cook time 25 minutes **makes** 8
nutritional count per skewer 1.4g total fat
(0.2g saturated fat); 163kJ (39 cal);
4.8g carbohydrate; 1.3g protein; 1.5g fibre

dukkah beetroot and kumara skewers

Cut 1 medium kumara (orange sweet potato) into 2.5cm (1 inch) pieces. Boil, steam or microwave kumara until tender; drain. Drain 440g (14 ounces) canned baby beetroot (beets). Thread kumara and beetroot onto 8 bamboo skewers; cook skewers on heated oiled barbecue (or grill or grill pan) about 10 minutes or until tender. Meanwhile, combine 2 tablespoons olive oil, 2 tablespoons white wine vinegar and 1 tablespoon finely chopped fresh mint in small jug; season to taste. Serve skewers drizzled with mint dressing; sprinkle with 1 tablespoon dukkah.

prep + cook time 35 minutes **makes** 8
nutritional count per skewer 5.9g total fat
(0.8g saturated fat); 426kJ (102 cal);
9.7g carbohydrate; 1.7g protein; 2g fibre

notes We used almond dukkah, available from the spice section of larger supermarkets.

grilled sweet potato salad

1 small kumara (orange sweet potato) (250g),
unpeeled, sliced thickly
1 small purple sweet potato (250g), unpeeled,
sliced thickly
1 small white sweet potato (250g), unpeeled,
sliced thickly
2 tablespoons coarsely chopped fresh
flat-leaf parsley
¼ cup (35g) macadamias, roasted,
chopped coarsely

SHERRY VINEGAR DRESSING
2 tablespoons sherry vinegar
2 tablespoons macadamia (or olive) oil

1 Boil, steam or microwave sweet potatoes until
almost tender; drain.
2 Meanwhile, make sherry vinegar dressing.
3 Cook potatoes on heated oiled barbecue
(or grill or grill pan) until browned.
4 Place potatoes on serving platter. Drizzle
with dressing; sprinkle with parsley and nuts.

SHERRY VINEGAR DRESSING Combine ingredients
in screw-top jar; shake well, season to taste.

prep + cook time 30 minutes **serves** 4
nutritional count per serving 16.1g total fat
(2.2g saturated fat); 1187kJ (284 cal);
28.8g carbohydrate; 4g protein; 4.1g fibre

caramelised fig, orange and fennel salad

6 medium figs (360g), halved
1 medium fennel bulb (300g), trimmed
90g (3 ounces) mesclun
2 large oranges (300g), segmented

ORANGE AND HONEY DRESSING
1 teaspoon finely grated orange rind
2 tablespoons orange juice
1 tablespoon honey
1 tablespoon olive oil

1 Make orange and honey dressing.
2 Place figs and dressing in large bowl; turn gently to coat. Remove figs from dressing; reserve dressing.
3 Cook figs on heated oiled barbecue (or grill or grill pan) until caramelised.
4 Using a mandolin, V-slicer or sharp knife, slice fennel thinly. Add mesclun, fennel and orange to bowl with dressing; toss gently to combine. Place salad on serving platter; top with figs.

ORANGE AND HONEY DRESSING Combine ingredients in screw-top jar; shake well, season to taste.

prep + cook time 25 minutes **serves** 4
nutritional count per serving 4.9g total fat (0.6g saturated fat); 594kJ (142 cal); 19.9g carbohydrate; 2.5g protein; 4.8g fibre

ginger squid with apple and celery coleslaw

625g (1¼ pounds) cleaned squid hoods
1 teaspoon sesame oil
4cm (1½ inch) piece fresh ginger (20g), grated
2 teaspoons sambal oelek
2 stalks celery (450g), trimmed
2 medium apples (300g)
2 cups (160g) finely shredded cabbage
2 green onions (scallions), sliced thinly
½ cup finely chopped fresh mint
½ cup finely chopped fresh coriander (cilantro)

LEMON DRESSING
2 tablespoons lemon juice
2 teaspoons dijon mustard
1 tablespoon peanut oil

1 Cut squid down centre to open out; score inside in a diagonal pattern, then cut into thick strips. Combine squid, oil, ginger and sambal in medium bowl.
2 Make lemon dressing.
3 Cut celery into 8cm lengths. Cut apples and celery lengthways into thin slices, then cut slices into matchstick-sized pieces. Combine celery, apple, cabbage, onion, herbs and dressing in large bowl.
4 Cook squid on heated oiled barbecue (or grill or grill pan) until changed in colour. Serve squid with coleslaw.

LEMON DRESSING Combine ingredients in screw-top jar; shake well, season to taste.

prep + cook time 40 minutes serves 4
nutritional count per serving 7.9g total fat (1.6g saturated fat); 974kJ (233 cal); 10.8g carbohydrate; 27.6g protein; 4.2g fibre

barbecued red onion, capsicum and goat's cheese with mint chimichurri

4 medium red onions (680g), cut into wedges
450g (14 ounce) jar roasted red capsicums (bell peppers), drained, chopped coarsely
220g (7 ounces) goat's cheese, crumbled

MINT CHIMICHURRI
1 cup loosely packed fresh mint leaves, chopped coarsely
1 small green capsicum (bell pepper) (150g), seeded, chopped coarsely
¾ cup (180ml) avocado or light olive oil
1 fresh long green chilli, sliced thinly
1 teaspoon ground cumin

1 Make mint chimichurri.
2 Cook onion on heated oiled barbecue (or grill or grill pan) until just tender.
3 Combine onion, capsicum and cheese in large bowl; season to taste.
4 Serve salad drizzled with chimichurri.

MINT CHIMICHURRI Blend or process half the mint with capsicum, oil, chilli and cumin until finely chopped. Transfer to small bowl; stir in remaining mint, season to taste.

prep + cook time 35 minutes **serves** 4
nutritional count per serving 52.8g total fat (11.5g saturated fat); 2437kJ (583 cal); 14.6g carbohydrate; 12g protein; 4.7g fibre

Chimichurri is a spicy marinade and dipping sauce often served with grilled meat; it is popular in many Latin and South American countries, especially Argentina.

charred pear, celery and walnut salad with tarragon pesto

2 stalks celery (300g), trimmed
4 small corella pears (400g), sliced thinly lengthways
1 small red capsicum (bell pepper) (150g), seeded, chopped finely
1 cup firmly packed fresh celery leaves
½ cup walnuts (50g), roasted, chopped coarsely

TARRAGON PESTO
1 cup firmly packed fresh tarragon leaves
2 slices (90g) white bread, crusts removed
¼ cup (60ml) milk
¼ cup (60ml) water
2 tablespoons olive oil
1 teaspoon sea salt

1   Make tarragon pesto.
2   Cut celery into 8cm pieces; cut pieces lengthways into matchstick-sized pieces.
3   Cook pear on heated oiled barbecue (or grill or grill pan) until browned lightly both sides.
4   Combine celery, pear, capsicum, celery leaves, nuts and ¼ cup of the tarragon pesto in large bowl; season to taste.
5   Serve salad drizzled with remaining pesto.

TARRAGON PESTO   Blend or process ingredients until smooth.

prep + cook time 30 minutes serves 4
nutritional count per serving 18.9g total fat
(2.3g saturated fat); 1162kJ (278 cal);
21.1g carbohydrate; 4.7g protein; 5.2g fibre

notes Use the yellow and lighter green leaves from the heart of the celery.
Add sliced blue cheese or brie to the salad, if you like.

grilled sardine and cherry tomato salad

18 fresh sardine fillets (800g)
250g (8 ounces) cherry truss tomatoes
2 teaspoons olive oil
90g (3 ounces) mixed salad leaves
1 tablespoon balsamic vinegar

HERB DRESSING
1 tablespoon lemon juice
2 tablespoons dry white wine
2 teaspoons olive oil
2 teaspoons each finely chopped fresh flat-leaf
  parsley and coriander (cilantro)
1 clove garlic, crushed

1 Make herb dressing.
2 Thread 18 skewers with one sardine fillet each, weaving diagonally through each fillet to secure.
3 Drizzle tomatoes with oil; season. Cook on heated oiled barbecue (or grill or grill pan) until tomatoes soften.
4 Cook sardines, skin-side down, without turning, on heated oiled barbecue, drizzling with half the herb dressing during cooking.
5 Toss salad leaves with vinegar in large bowl. Drizzle sardines with remaining dressing; serve with salad leaves and tomatoes.

HERB DRESSING Combine ingredients in screw-top jar; shake well, season to taste.

prep + cook time 35 minutes serves 6
nutritional count per serving 11.8g total fat
(2.7g saturated fat); 828kJ (198 cal);
1.3g carbohydrate; 19.9g protein; 1g fibre

Soak bamboo skewers in cold water for at least 30 minutes prior to using to prevent them from scorching during cooking.

balsamic-glazed vegetables

15 zucchini flowers with stems attached (150g),
   trimmed (see note)
4 baby fennel bulbs (520g), trimmed,
   cut into wedges
4 baby eggplants (240g), halved lengthways,
   score skin diagonally
1 large red capsicum (bell pepper) (350g), seeded,
   chopped coarsely
1 large yellow capsicum (bell pepper) (350g),
   seeded, chopped coarsely
⅓ cup (80ml) olive oil
2 small radicchio (300g), trimmed, chopped coarsely
¼ cup (60ml) balsamic glaze

1 Remove stamens from centre of zucchini
flowers. Brush fennel, eggplant, capsicum and
zucchini flowers and stems with oil.
2 Cook vegetables, in batches, on heated oiled
barbecue (or grill or grill pan) until tender; transfer
to large bowl, cover to keep warm.
3 Add radicchio and balsamic glaze to vegetables;
toss gently, season to taste.

prep + cook time 35 minutes **serves** 6
nutritional count per serving 12.7g total fat
(1.7g saturated fat); 686kJ (164 cal);
6.9g carbohydrate; 3.4g protein; 4.7g fibre

note The stem of the zucchini is the baby zucchini
attached to the flower.

thai barbecued beef salad

500g (1 pound) beef rump steak
125g (4 ounces) rice vermicelli noodles
250g (8 ounces) cherry truss tomatoes
1 lebanese cucumber (130g), seeded, sliced thinly
1 cup (80g) bean sprouts
1 cup each loosely packed fresh mint leaves and
   coriander (cilantro) leaves

SWEET AND SOUR DRESSING
¼ cup (60ml) lime juice
2 tablespoons grated palm sugar
1 tablespoon each fish sauce and light soy sauce
1 tablespoon peanut oil
1 clove garlic, crushed
2 fresh small red thai (serrano) chillies,
   chopped finely
1cm (½ inch) piece fresh ginger (5g), grated

1 Make sweet and sour dressing.
2 Combine steak and 2 tablespoons of the dressing
in large bowl.
3 Place noodles in large heatproof bowl, cover
with boiling water. Stand until tender; drain. Rinse
under cold water; drain.
4 Drain steak; cook on heated oiled barbecue (or
grill or grill pan). Remove steak from barbecue;
cover, stand 10 minutes then slice thinly.
5 Cook tomatoes on heated oiled barbecue
(or grill or grill pan) until skins begin to burst.
6 Combine noodles, steak, tomatoes, remaining
dressing and remaining ingredients in large bowl.

SWEET AND SOUR DRESSING Combine
ingredients in screw-top jar; shake well, season.

prep + cook time 35 minutes **serves** 4
nutritional count per serving 10.8g total fat
(3.4g saturated fat); 1221kJ (292 cal);
16.5g carbohydrate; 30.2g protein; 3.3g fibre

scallop and rocket salad

12 scallops without roe (300g)
75g (2½ ounces) baby rocket leaves (arugula)
1 lebanese cucumber (130g), sliced thinly
1 tablespoon sesame seeds, toasted
1 lime, cut into wedges

BALSAMIC DRESSING
1 tablespoon balsamic vinegar
1 teaspoon each olive oil and lime juice
pinch white sugar

1 Make balsamic dressing.
2 Pat scallops dry on absorbent paper. Cook scallops on heated oiled barbecue (or grill or grill pan) until browned lightly both sides. Remove from barbecue; cover to keep warm.
3 Combine rocket, cucumber and dressing in medium bowl. Top salad with scallops and sesame seeds. Serve with lime wedges.

BALSAMIC DRESSING Combine ingredients in screw-top jar; shake well, season to taste.

prep + cook time 15 minutes serves 4
nutritional count per serving 3.1g total fat (0.4g saturated fat); 222kJ (53 cal); 1.3g carbohydrate; 4.5g protein; 0.8g fibre

prawn, strawberry and poppy seed salad

18 uncooked medium king prawns (shrimp) (1kg)
185g (6 ounces) mixed salad leaves
500g (1 pound) strawberries, halved
90g (3 ounces) fetta cheese, crumbled
1 medium brown onion (150g), sliced thinly

POPPY SEED DRESSING
1½ tablespoons cider vinegar
1 tablespoon white sugar
½ teaspoon mustard powder
¾ cup (180ml) vegetable oil
2 teaspoons poppy seeds

1 Make poppy seed dressing.
2 Shell and devein prawns, leaving tails intact.
3 Cook prawns on heated oiled barbecue (or grill or grill pan) until changed in colour.
4 Combine salad leaves, strawberries, cheese, onion and half the poppy seed dressing in large bowl. Serve salad topped with prawns; drizzle with remaining dressing.

POPPY SEED DRESSING Blend or process vinegar, sugar and mustard until combined. With motor operating, gradually add oil in a thin, steady stream. Transfer to bowl, stir in seeds; season to taste.

prep + cook time 30 minutes **serves** 6
nutritional count per serving 32.3g total fat (5.9g saturated fat); 1710kJ (409 cal); 6.9g carbohydrate; 22g protein; 2.7g fibre

haloumi, asparagus and red onion skewers

Combine ½ cup balsamic vinegar, 1 tablespoon honey and 1 tablespoon light brown sugar in small saucepan; stir over low heat, without boiling, until sugar dissolves. Bring to the boil; boil, uncovered, about 5 minutes or until syrup thickens slightly, cool. Meanwhile, cut 350g (11 ounces) haloumi cheese and 150g (5 ounces) asparagus into 2.5cm (1 inch) pieces; cut 1 small red onion into thin wedges. Thread cheese, asparagus and onion onto 8 bamboo skewers; season. Cook skewers on heated oiled barbecue (or grill or grill pan) until browned and tender. Serve skewers immediately, drizzled with balsamic syrup.

prep + cook time 35 minutes **makes** 8
nutritional count per skewer 7.8g total fat
(4.8g saturated fat); 564kJ (135 cal);
6.1g carbohydrate; 9.8g protein; 0.4g fibre

note Thick asparagus is best for this recipe.

barbecued red curry vegetable skewers

Coarsely chop 1 medium red capsicum (bell pepper). Halve 1 large zucchini lengthways; chop coarsely. Halve 12 button mushrooms. Thread vegetables onto 8 skewers; brush skewers all over with 2 tablespoons red curry paste. Cook skewers on heated oiled barbecue (or grill or grill pan) about 15 minutes or until vegetables are tender. Meanwhile, cook 2 tablespoons red curry paste in heated small saucepan, stirring, about 5 minutes or until fragrant. Add 1 cup coconut milk; bring to the boil. Reduce heat; simmer, uncovered, about 5 minutes or until mixture is thickened slightly, season to taste. Serve skewers drizzled with curry sauce; sprinkle with 2 tablespoons coarsely chopped fresh coriander (cilantro).

prep + cook time 35 minutes **makes** 8
nutritional count per skewer 10.8g total fat
(6.1g saturated fat); 523kJ (125 cal);
3.5g carbohydrate; 2.5g protein; 2.8g fibre

serving suggestion Lime wedges and steamed jasmine rice.

barbecued corn on the cob with tahini

Remove silk from 4 whole corn cobs, leaving husks intact. Soak corn cobs in water for 15 minutes. Meanwhile, combine 45g (1½ ounces) softened butter, 1½ tablespoons tahini, ½ teaspoon cayenne pepper and 2 teaspoons finely chopped fresh coriander (cilantro) in small bowl. Peel back corn husks carefully; brush butter mixture all over corn then carefully fold husks back over corn. Tie tops with string or secure with small piece of foil. Cook corn on heated barbecue (or grill or grill pan) about 15 minutes, turning regularly to cook evenly. Peel husks from corn, cut cobs in half.

prep + cook time 40 minutes **serves** 8
nutritional count per serving 8.6g total fat (3.5g saturated fat); 903kJ (216 cal); 24g carbohydrate; 6.9g protein; 7.1g fibre

balsamic mushrooms with fetta crumble

Combine 125g (4 ounces) crumbled fetta cheese in small bowl with 1 seeded, finely chopped large tomato, ¼ cup finely chopped fresh basil and 2 tablespoons olive oil. Trim the stalks of 8 flat mushrooms; drizzle mushrooms with 2 tablespoons balsamic vinegar combined with 1 tablespoon oil. Cook mushrooms on heated oiled barbecue (or grill or grill pan) until tender. Transfer to serving plate; top with fetta mixture.

prep + cook time 30 minutes **serves** 4
nutritional count per serving 21.4g total fat (6.7g saturated fat); 1083kJ (259 cal); 2.9g carbohydrate; 11.6g protein; 4.3g fibre

honey mustard baby carrots with silver beet

750g (1½ pounds) baby carrots, peeled, trimmed
2 tablespoons olive oil
2 teaspoons each ground cumin and mild paprika
1 small bunch (250g) silver beet (swiss chard),
 trimmed, shredded finely
5 shallots (125g), sliced thinly

HONEY MUSTARD DRESSING
⅓ cup (80ml) olive oil
2 tablespoons cider vinegar
1 teaspoon dijonnaise
1 tablespoon honey

1 Make honey mustard dressing.
2 Combine carrots, oil and spices in large bowl.
Cook carrots on heated oiled barbecue (or grill or
grill pan) until tender.
3 Combine silver beet and shallot in large bowl
with carrots and dressing; season to taste.

HONEY MUSTARD DRESSING Combine
ingredients in small screw-top jar; shake well,
season to taste.

prep + cook time 35 minutes **serves** 4
nutritional count per serving 27.6g total fat
(3.9g saturated fat); 1371kJ (328 cal);
15.8g carbohydrate; 2.3g protein; 5.7g fibre

grilled asparagus and mushrooms with anchovy dressing

4 large flat mushrooms (320g)
170g (5½ ounces) asparagus
1 tablespoon olive oil
½ small red onion (50g), sliced thinly

ANCHOVY DRESSING
3 anchovies, drained, chopped finely
2 tablespoons finely chopped fresh
  flat-leaf parsley
3 cloves garlic, crushed
2 tablespoons lemon juice
¼ cup (60ml) olive oil

1   Make anchovy dressing.
2   Brush mushrooms and asparagus with oil; cook on heated oiled barbecue (or grill or grill pan) until tender, brushing with half the anchovy dressing during cooking.
3   Top vegetables with remaining dressing; serve with onion.

ANCHOVY DRESSING Combine ingredients in screw-top jar; shake well, season to taste.

prep + cook time 20 minutes **serves** 4
nutritional count per serving 18.8g total fat (2.6g saturated fat); 857kJ (205 cal); 2.8g carbohydrate; 4.8g protein; 3.1g fibre

seafood

chilli marinated prawns with aïoli

24 large uncooked king prawns (shrimp) (1.7kg)
¼ cup (60ml) olive oil
3 cloves garlic, crushed
1 tablespoon finely chopped fresh coriander
  (cilantro)
2 fresh small red thai (serrano) chillies,
  chopped finely
1 teaspoon each ground cumin and paprika
1 teaspoon honey
1 tablespoon lime juice
1 cos (romaine) lettuce, torn
2 lebanese cucumbers (260g), peeled, halved,
  sliced thinly
1 medium avocado (250g), chopped coarsely
2 tablespoons olive oil, extra
2 teaspoons lemon juice

AÏOLI
1 medium garlic bulb (70g)
⅔ cup (200g) whole-egg mayonnaise

1 Shell and devein prawns leaving tails intact.
2 Combine prawns, oil, garlic, coriander, chilli,
spices, honey and lime juice in medium bowl.
Cover, refrigerate 30 minutes.
3 Meanwhile, make aïoli.
4 Remove prawns from marinade; cook on heated
oiled barbecue (or grill or grill pan).
5 Combine lettuce, cucumber and avocado in
medium bowl; drizzle with combined extra oil and
juice. Season to taste.
6 Serve prawns with salad and aïoli.

AÏOLI Preheat oven to 180°C/350°F. Cut top
off garlic bulb. Drizzle bulb with a little olive oil;
wrap in foil. Roast in small baking dish, uncovered,
about 25 minutes or until tender; cool. Squeeze
garlic from each clove; mash to a paste in a small
bowl. Mix in mayonnaise; season to taste.

prep + cook time 45 minutes (+ refrigeration)
serves 6
nutritional count per serving 34g total fat
(4.9g saturated fat); 2040kJ (488 cal);
11.5g carbohydrate; 32.4g protein; 4.8g fibre

tuna kebabs with soy and wasabi

Cut 1kg (2 pounds) thick tuna steaks into 2.5cm (1 inch) cubes. Combine tuna, ½ cup firmly packed light brown sugar, ¼ cup light soy sauce, 2 tablespoons wasabi paste and 1 tablespoon sesame oil in large bowl. Thread three cubes of tuna onto each skewer. Cook kebabs and halved limes on heated oiled barbecue (or grill or grill pan).

prep + cook time 25 minutes **makes** 10
nutritional count per kebab 8.1g total fat
(2.8g saturated fat); 874kJ (209 cal);
8.6g carbohydrate; 25.5g protein; 0.1g fibre

prawn and scallop kebabs with peri peri

Shell and devein 16 medium king prawns (shrimp) leaving tails intact. Remove roe from 16 scallops. Combine prawns and scallops with ¼ cup mustard seed oil and 2 tablespoons peri peri seasoning in large bowl. Thread scallops and prawns alternately onto skewers. Cook on heated oiled barbecue (or grill or grill plate). Serve with lemon wedges.

prep + cook time 30 minutes **makes** 8
nutritional count per kebab 7.9g total fat
(1g saturated fat); 535kJ (128 cal);
0.6g carbohydrate; 13g protein; 0.6g fibre

sardine skewers with gremolata dressing

Make gremolata dressing by combining 1 cup firmly packed fresh flat-leaf parsley leaves, chopped coarsely, ⅓ cup coarsely chopped preserved lemon rind, ¼ cup mustard seed oil and 4 crushed garlic cloves in small bowl. Meanwhile, thread 10 butterflied sardine fillets onto metal skewers; cook on heated oiled barbecue (or grill or grill pan). Season; serve with dressing.

prep + cook time 35 minutes **makes** 10
nutritional count per skewer 9g total fat
(1.6g saturated fat); 464kJ (111 cal);
0.3g carbohydrate; 6.9g protein; 0.7g fibre

rosemary, basil and garlic cuttlefish skewers

Cut 5 cleaned small cuttlefish or calamari hoods in half lengthways; score inside in diagonal pattern. Combine cuttlefish with ¼ cup lemon-flavoured olive oil, 2 tablespoons each finely chopped fresh rosemary and basil, 2 crushed garlic cloves, 2 teaspoons finely grated lemon rind and ¼ cup lemon juice in large bowl; season. Thread each piece of cuttlefish onto a bamboo skewer; cook on heated oiled barbecue (or grill or grill pan).

prep + cook time 30 minutes **makes** 10
nutritional count per skewer 6.4g total fat
(1g saturated fat); 418kJ (100 cal);
0.2g carbohydrate; 10.1g protein; 0.1g fibre

yogurt marinated fish with herb and watercress salad

½ cup (140g) plain yogurt
2 cloves garlic, crushed
4cm (1½ inch) piece fresh ginger (20g), grated
2 teaspoons ground coriander
1 teaspoon garam masala
4 firm white fish fillets (600g), skin on
3 cups loosely packed watercress sprigs, trimmed
½ cup loosely packed fresh coriander
   (cilantro) leaves
½ cup loosely packed fresh mint leaves
½ small red onion (50g), sliced thinly
2 tablespoons lime juice

1 Combine yogurt, garlic, ginger, spices and fish in medium bowl. Cover, refrigerate 3 hours.
2 Remove fish from marinade; discard marinade. Cook fish on heated oiled barbecue flat plate.
3 Meanwhile, combine remaining ingredients in large bowl; season to taste. Serve fish with herb salad; accompany with lime wedges.

prep + cook time 30 minutes (+ refrigeration)
serves 4
nutritional count per serving 4.8g total fat (1.6g saturated fat); 836kJ (200 cal); 3.5g carbohydrate; 33.8g protein; 1.9g fibre

notes We used blue-eye fillets for this recipe, but any white fish fillet will be fine.
You need to buy a 350g bunch of watercress.

We used swordfish steaks, but any firm white fish will be fine.

fish with fennel and lemon mint vinaigrette

2 medium fennel bulbs (600g)
1 tablespoon olive oil
2 tablespoons lemon juice
⅓ cup firmly packed fresh mint leaves,
  chopped finely
1 tablespoon white wine vinegar
4 white fish steaks (750g)

1 Discard stalk from fennel; cut bulb into quarters and remove core.
2 Combine oil, juice, mint and vinegar in small bowl. Brush fennel with some of the oil mixture. Cook fennel on heated oiled barbecue (or grill or grill pan) about 10 minutes, turning often.
3 Meanwhile, brush fish with some of the oil mixture. Cook on heated oiled barbecue, brushing with more oil mixture during cooking.
4 Serve fish and fennel drizzled with remaining oil mixture; season.

prep + cook time 25 minutes **serves** 4
nutritional count per serving 8.8g total fat
(2g saturated fat); 1074kJ (257 cal);
3.2g carbohydrate; 39.3g protein; 2.7g fibre

serving suggestion Serve with a green salad and grilled cherry tomatoes.

seafood salad with salsa verde

500g (1 pound) large uncooked king prawns (shrimp)
250g (½ pound) scallops, roe removed
500g (1 pound) cleaned whole baby octopus, halved
500g (1 pound) large black mussels
90g (3 ounces) baby spinach leaves

SALSA VERDE
⅔ cup finely chopped fresh flat-leaf parsley
½ cup finely chopped fresh mint
½ cup finely chopped fresh basil
2 cloves garlic, chopped finely
1 tablespoon rinsed, drained capers,
  chopped finely
3 drained anchovy fillets, chopped finely
¼ cup (60ml) olive oil
1 tablespoon red wine vinegar
1 teaspoon dijon mustard

1   Make salsa verde.
2   Shell and devein prawns leaving tails intact.
Combine prawns, scallops and octopus in large
bowl with half the salsa verde.
3   Scrub mussels, remove beards; cook mussels
on heated oiled barbecue plate (or grill or grill pan)
until mussels open (discard any that don't). Remove
from heat.
4   Add prawn mixture to heated oiled barbecue
plate; cook, turning, until mixture is cooked.
5   Serve seafood on spinach; drizzle with remaining
salsa verde.

SALSA VERDE   Combine ingredients in medium
bowl; season to taste.

prep + cook time 45 minutes serves 4
nutritional count per serving 17.9g total fat
(2.8g saturated fat); 1626kJ (389 cal);
3.6g carbohydrate; 52.2g protein; 2g fibre

serving suggestion Serve salad with lemon
wedges and toasted bread.

toasted tuna sandwiches with pineapple and avocado salsa

4 tuna steaks (400g)
8 slices sourdough bread
1 tablespoon olive oil
2 lebanese cucumbers (260g), sliced thinly
  lengthways

PINEAPPLE AND AVOCADO SALSA
¼ small pineapple (220g) chopped finely
½ small red onion (50g), chopped finely
1 fresh small red thai (serrano) chilli, chopped finely
1 tablespoon finely chopped fresh basil
1 tablespoon lime juice
1 medium avocado (250g), diced finely

1 Season fish; stand at room temperature 5 minutes.
2 Meanwhile, make pineapple and avocado salsa.
3 Brush one side of bread slices with oil. Toast slices, oiled-side down, on heated barbecue (or grill or grill pan).
4 Cook fish on heated oiled barbecue about 2 minutes each side.
5 Sandwich cucumber, fish and salsa between toasted bread.

PINEAPPLE AND AVOCADO SALSA Combine ingredients in medium bowl; season to taste.

prep + cook time 25 minutes serves 4
nutritional count per serving 22.6g total fat (5.4g saturated fat); 2040kJ (488 cal); 35.6g carbohydrate; 32.7g protein; 5.3g fibre

dukkah fish in vine leaves

¼ cup (35g) dukkah
8 large whole garfish (1kg), cleaned
8 vine leaves in brine, rinsed, drained
⅓ cup (80ml) lemon juice

CAPSICUM AND CAPER SALAD
2 small red capsicums (bell peppers) (300g),
  sliced thickly
1 tablespoon lemon juice
1 tablespoon olive oil
1 clove garlic, crushed
1 small red onion (100g), sliced thinly
1 tablespoon rinsed, drained baby capers
⅓ cup (50g) seeded black olives
90g (3 ounces) baby rocket leaves (arugula)

1 Make capsicum and caper salad.
2 Sprinkle half the dukkah into fish cavities.
3 Pat vine leaves dry with absorbent paper. Lay vine leaves, rib-side up, on bench. Place one garfish on each leaf; sprinkle with remaining dukkah, drizzle with juice. Wrap vine leaf around fish to enclose, leaving tails exposed.
4 Cook fish on heated oiled barbecue (or grill or grill pan). Serve fish with salad.

CAPSICUM AND CAPER SALAD Cook capsicum on heated oiled barbecue (or grill or grill pan) until tender. Combine juice, oil and garlic in screw-top jar; shake well. Combine capsicum, dressing and remaining ingredients in large bowl; season to taste.

prep + cook time 30 minutes serves 4
nutritional count per serving 11.8g total fat (1.8g saturated fat); 1150kJ (275 cal); 8.5g carbohydrate; 31.6g protein; 2.8g fibre

note If you can't get garfish, whiting or large sardines are also fine to use.

prawns with chilli mango dressing

2 tablespoons each black and sichuan peppercorns
2 teaspoons sea salt
2 tablespoons cornflour (cornstarch)
1 teaspoon mild paprika
20 medium uncooked king prawns (shrimp) (900g)
125g (4 ounces) baby spinach leaves

CHILLI MANGO DRESSING
1 tablespoon white sugar
1 tablespoon water
2 small mangoes (600g), chopped coarsely
2 tablespoons lemon juice
1 tablespoon fish sauce
2 fresh small red thai (serrano) chillies,
  chopped finely

1 Make chilli mango dressing.
2 Dry-fry peppercorns and salt in small frying pan over medium heat until fragrant. Pound in mortar and pestle until coarse.
3 Combine spice mix, cornflour and paprika in medium bowl.
4 Shell and devein prawns leaving tails intact. Add prawns to spice mixture; mix well.
5 Cook prawns on heated oiled barbecue (or grill or grill pan). Serve with spinach; drizzle with dressing.

CHILLI MANGO DRESSING Combine sugar and the water in small saucepan; stir over heat until sugar dissolves. Bring to the boil; reduce heat, simmer about 1 minute without stirring until liquid is reduced by half. Cool syrup 5 minutes. Blend syrup with remaining ingredients until combined.

prep + cook time 40 minutes serves 4
nutritional count per serving 1g total fat
(0.1g saturated fat); 782kJ (187 cal);
21.9g carbohydrate; 25.3g protein; 2.5g fibre

salmon with lime and coriander pesto

4 salmon fillets (640g), without skin
90g (3 ounces) baby spinach leaves
1 lebanese cucumber (130g), cut into thin ribbons
3 red radishes (110g), trimmed, sliced thinly

LIME AND CORIANDER PESTO
⅓ cup (50g) unsalted roasted cashews
1 fresh small red thai (serrano) chilli, chopped coarsely
1 cup firmly packed fresh coriander (cilantro) leaves
⅔ cup firmly packed fresh mint leaves
1 clove garlic, quartered
2 teaspoons finely grated lime rind
2 tablespoons each olive oil, lime juice and water

1 Make lime and coriander pesto.
2 Cook fish on heated oiled barbecue (or grill or grill pan) until almost cooked through.
3 Meanwhile, combine spinach, cucumber and radish in medium bowl.
4 Serve fish with spinach salad and pesto.

LIME AND CORIANDER PESTO Blend or process nuts, chilli, coriander, mint, garlic and rind until finely chopped. With motor operating, add oil in a thin, steady stream; blend mixture until combined. Stir in juice and the water.

prep + cook time 35 minutes serves 4
nutritional count per serving 27.4g total fat
(5g saturated fat); 1689kJ (404 cal);
3.8g carbohydrate; 34.6g protein; 2.7g fibre

warm octopus and olive salad

1kg cleaned baby octopus
3 cloves garlic, sliced thinly
½ cup finely chopped fresh flat-leaf parsley
3 teaspoons dried oregano leaves
½ small red onion (50g), chopped finely
3 fresh bay leaves
2 tablespoons olive oil
1 tablespoon finely grated lemon rind
¼ cup (60ml) lemon juice
½ cup (75g) seeded black olives
90g (3 ounces) mesclun
125g (4 ounces) grape tomatoes, halved

1 Place octopus in medium heatproof bowl. Pour boiling water over octopus to cover; stand 2 minutes, drain. Combine octopus in large bowl with garlic, parsley, oregano, onion, bay leaves, oil, rind and juice. Cover, refrigerate 30 minutes.
2 Cook olives on heated oiled barbecue plate (or grill or grill pan) until hot. Transfer to medium bowl with mesclun and tomatoes; toss gently.
3 Cook octopus on heated oiled barbecue plate; add to salad. Serve with lemon wedges.

prep + cook time 30 minutes (+ refrigeration)
serves 4
nutritional count per serving 14.4g total fat (2.4g saturated fat); 1793kJ (429 cal); 8.3g carbohydrate; 64.5g protein; 2g fibre

salmon kebabs with spiced chickpea dip

1kg (2 pounds) thick salmon fillets or steaks
⅓ cup (80ml) olive oil
1 tablespoon sumac
410g (13 ounces) canned chickpeas (garbanzo),
  rinsed, drained
2 tablespoons coarsely chopped fresh
  flat-leaf parsley
1 tablespoon ground cumin
½ cup (125ml) cold water

1 Cut salmon into 4cm (1½ inch) cubes; thread 3 cubes onto each skewer.
2 Combine skewers, 2 tablespoons of the oil and sumac in large shallow dish. Cover, refrigerate 1 hour.
3 Meanwhile, blend or process chickpeas, parsley, cumin, remaining oil and the water until smooth; season to taste.
4 Cook skewers on heated oiled barbecue (or grill or grill pan). Serve with spiced chickpea dip.

prep + cook time 25 minutes (+ refrigeration)
makes 10
nutritional count per skewer 15.2g total fat
(2.7g saturated fat); 991kJ (237 cal);
3.7g carbohydrate; 21.2g protein; 1.3g fibre

thai fish cake skewers

1kg (2 pounds) boneless white fish fillets
2 tablespoons red curry paste
1 egg
2 shallots (50g) chopped finely
2 tablespoons finely chopped fresh coriander
  (cilantro)
2 fresh small red thai (serrano) chillies, sliced thinly
2 teaspoons finely grated lime rind
2 tablespoons lime juice

1 Blend or process fish, paste and egg until combined. Transfer mixture to large bowl, mix in shallot, coriander, chilli, rind and juice; season.
2 Roll rounded tablespoons of mixture into balls. Thread 3 balls onto each skewer.
3 Cook fish cakes, flattening slightly, on heated oiled barbecue (or grill or grill pan). Serve skewers with lime wedges and sweet chilli sauce.

prep + cook time 35 minutes **makes** 8
nutritional count per skewer 7.4g total fat (1.8g saturated fat); 911kJ (218 cal); 1g carbohydrate; 35.9g protein; 1g fibre

note The fish cake mixture can be covered and refrigerated for 2 hours or overnight before cooking.

poultry

cajun chicken burgers with lemon yogurt

2 chicken breast fillets (400g)
2 tablespoons cajun seasoning
4 crusty bread rolls
⅓ cup (95g) yogurt
2 teaspoons finely grated lemon rind
1 medium tomato (150g), chopped finely
1 shallot (25g), chopped finely
½ small ripe avocado (100g), chopped finely
50g mesclun

1   Cut chicken in half horizontally; sprinkle all over with seasoning. Cook on heated oiled barbecue (or grill or grill pan).
2   Meanwhile, cut rolls in half; toast, cut-sides down, on barbecue.
3   Combine yogurt and rind in small bowl.
4   Combine tomato, shallot and avocado in small bowl; season.
5   Sandwich mesclun, avocado mixture, chicken and yogurt mixture between rolls.

prep + cook time 30 minutes **serves** 4
nutritional count per serving 12.9g total fat (3.3g saturated fat); 1731kJ (414 cal); 41.8g carbohydrate; 30.2g protein; 3.7g fibre

note For fish burgers, replace the chicken with four firm white fish fillets (125g/4 ounces each).

spiced plum chicken kebabs

Combine 250g (8 ounces) drained and seeded canned plums in syrup, 1 tablespoon each honey and dark soy sauce, 1 teaspoon worcestershire sauce, ½ teaspoon Tabasco sauce and ¼ teaspoon ground cardamom in medium saucepan. Bring to the boil, simmer, uncovered, 5 minutes; cool then blend or process until smooth. Season to taste. Cut 750g (1½ pounds) chicken breast fillets into cubes; thread onto 12 skewers. Cook skewers on heated oiled barbecue (or grill or grill pan), basting occasionally with some of the plum sauce. Serve skewers with remaining sauce.

prep + cook time 35 minutes **makes** 12
nutritional count per skewer 2.6g total fat (0.8g saturated fat); 330kJ (79 cal); 3.7g carbohydrate; 10.2g protein; 0.1g fibre

chicken tikka kebabs with spicy yogurt

Cut 750g (1½ pounds) chicken breast fillets into cubes; combine in large bowl with 1 cup yogurt, 1 tablespoon lemon juice, 2 teaspoons ground cumin, 1 teaspoon each ground cinnamon and cracked black pepper, ½ teaspoon cayenne pepper and 2 crushed garlic cloves. Cover, refrigerate 1 hour. Cut 1 medium brown onion into wedges. Thread chicken and onion alternately onto 12 skewers, reserving marinade. Cook chicken on heated oiled barbecue (or grill or grill pan). Meanwhile, boil reserved marinade in small saucepan. Reduce heat, add 2 tablespoons tomato paste, ⅓ cup pouring cream and 1 tablespoon lemon juice; simmer, uncovered, until thickened slightly. Season to taste. Serve skewers with extra sauce.

prep + cook time 30 minutes (+ refrigeration)
makes 12
nutritional count per skewer 5.2g total fat (2.5g saturated fat); 423kJ (101 cal); 2.1g carbohydrate; 11.3g protein; 0.3g fibre

spicy yogurt chicken drumettes with raita

Combine 20 chicken drumettes in large bowl with ¾ cup yogurt, ½ teaspoon dried chilli flakes, 1 tablespoon each ground cumin and coriander and 2 teaspoons ground turmeric. Cover; refrigerate 30 minutes. Remove drumettes from marinade; shake off excess. Discard marinade. Cook drumettes on heated oiled barbecue (or grill or grill pan) until cooked through. Meanwhile, make raita by combining ½ cup each finely chopped fresh mint and fresh coriander (cilantro), ¾ cup yogurt, 1 crushed garlic clove and 1 tablespoon lemon juice in small bowl.

prep + cook time 35 minutes (+ refrigeration)
serves 4
nutritional count per serving 15.4g total fat (6.3g saturated fat); 1509kJ (361 cal); 7.9g carbohydrate; 46.4g protein; 0.6g fibre

vietnamese chicken rolls

Cook 8 chicken tenderloins on heated oiled barbecue (or grill or grill pan). Cut 1 small carrot, and 1 seeded lebanese cucumber into matchstick-sized pieces. Split 4 crusty long white bread rolls lengthways without cutting all the way through. Spread roll bases with ⅓ cup whole-egg mayonnaise; top with 1 cup shredded iceberg lettuce, chicken, carrot and cucumber. Drizzle with ¼ cup sweet chilli sauce and top with ½ cup loosely packed fresh coriander (cilantro) leaves.

prep + cook time 20 minutes **serves** 4
nutritional count per serving 19.6g total fat (3.9g saturated fat); 2253kJ (539 cal); 48.5g carbohydrate; 39.5g protein; 4.5g fibre

sticky sweet and sour quail

½ cup (125ml) balsamic vinegar
1 tablespoon honey
1 tablespoon light brown sugar
2 cloves garlic, crushed
1 fresh long red chilli, chopped finely
1 teaspoon fennel seeds
6 quails (960g)
1 tablespoon finely chopped fresh basil

PINE NUT SALAD
2 teaspoons olive oil
2 teaspoons balsamic vinegar
60g (2 ounces) baby rocket leaves (arugula)
1 cup loosely packed fresh basil leaves
1 lebanese cucumber (130g), seeded, sliced thinly
2 tablespoons roasted pine nuts

1 Combine vinegar, honey and sugar in small saucepan; stir over heat until sugar dissolves. Bring to the boil; boil, uncovered, about 5 minutes or until syrup thickens slightly. Remove from heat; stir in garlic, chilli and seeds. Transfer syrup to large heatproof bowl; cool.
2 Meanwhile, using scissors, cut along both sides of quails' backbones; discard backbones. Halve each quail along breastbone; cut each in half again to give 24 pieces.
3 Cook quail, covered, on heated oiled barbecue (or grill or grill pan), turning occasionally, about 20 minutes.
4 Add hot quail and basil to syrup; mix well.
5 Meanwhile, make pine nut salad. Serve quail with salad.

PINE NUT SALAD Whisk oil and vinegar in large bowl; add remaining ingredients, toss gently. Season to taste.

prep + cook time 1 hour serves 4
nutritional count per serving 20.8g total fat
(4.1g saturated fat); 1384kJ (331 cal);
10.6g carbohydrate; 24.2g protein; 1.6g fibre

chicken parcels

600g (1¼ pounds) kipfler potatoes,
  halved lengthways
4 x 155g (5 ounces) chicken breast fillets
½ cup (120g) ricotta cheese
150g (5 ounces) baby spinach leaves
⅓ cup (50g) drained semi-dried tomatoes in oil
100g (3½ ounces) shaved leg ham
1 clove garlic, crushed
1 tablespoon fresh lemon thyme leaves
1 tablespoon olive oil
1 tablespoon balsamic vinegar
1 lebanese cucumber (130g), halved lengthways,
  seeded, sliced thinly
1 small red onion (100g), sliced thinly

1 Boil, steam or microwave potatoes until
tender; drain.
2 Meanwhile, cut chicken in half horizontally
without cutting all the way through; open chicken
out flat. Layer cheese, then about a quarter of the
spinach, the tomatoes and ham over half of each
chicken breast; season. Fold to enclose filling;
tie with kitchen string to secure.
3 Cook chicken on heated oiled barbecue (or grill
or grill pan). Cover chicken; stand 5 minutes then
slice thickly.
4 Meanwhile, combine potatoes, garlic, thyme
and half the oil in medium bowl. Cook potatoes
on heated oiled barbecue (or grill or grill pan)
until browned lightly.
5 Whisk remaining oil and vinegar in large bowl;
add cucumber, onion and remaining spinach, toss
gently. Season to taste.
6 Serve chicken with potatoes and spinach salad.

prep + cook time 1 hour serves 4
nutritional count per serving 12.6g total fat
(4g saturated fat); 1810kJ (433 cal);
26.5g carbohydrate; 48.8g protein; 6.5g fibre

chicken sausages with tomato salad

750g (1½ pounds) minced (ground) chicken
½ cup (75g) drained sun-dried tomatoes in oil, chopped finely
1 teaspoon fennel seeds, roasted
½ cup finely chopped fresh flat-leaf parsley
1 egg
½ cup (50g) packaged breadcrumbs
90g (3 ounces) baby spinach leaves
125g (4 ounces) cherry tomatoes, halved
½ cup (75g) fetta-stuffed green olives
2 teaspoons sherry vinegar
2 teaspoons olive oil

1   Combine mince, tomato, seeds, parsley, egg and breadcrumbs in large bowl. Shape mixture into 12 sausages.
2   Cook sausages on heated oiled barbecue flat plate (or grill).
3   Meanwhile, combine remaining ingredients in large bowl; season to taste.
4   Serve sausages with salad.

prep + cook time 30 minutes **serves** 4
nutritional count per serving 22.6g total fat (5.8g saturated fat); 1885kJ (451 cal); 15.8g carbohydrate; 42.6g protein; 6.1g fibre

tip To toast fennel seeds, place in a small dry frying pan over medium-low heat. Stir 1 minute or until fragrant.

spicy chicken with orange and watermelon salad

2 medium oranges (480g)
4 chicken thigh cutlets (800g), skin removed
2 tablespoons harissa sauce
2 cloves garlic, crushed
1 tablespoon olive oil
750g (1½ pound) piece watermelon, sliced thickly
⅓ cup coarsely chopped fresh mint
¼ cup (35g) coarsely chopped roasted
   unsalted pistachios
200g (6½ ounces) soft fetta cheese

1   Finely grate 2 teaspoons rind from oranges; segment oranges over small bowl to reserve juice.
2   Combine rind, chicken, sauce, garlic and oil in medium bowl; season.

3   Cook chicken on heated oiled covered barbecue (or grill or grill pan).
4   Meanwhile, combine orange segments, reserved juice, watermelon, mint and nuts in medium bowl; crumble cheese over salad. Serve chicken with salad and lime wedges.

prep + cook time 45 minutes **serves** 4
nutritional count per serving 35.7g total fat (13.3g saturated fat); 2466kJ (590 cal); 16.5g carbohydrate; 49.3g protein; 4.2g fibre

note Harissa is a fiery Moroccan sauce or paste made from dried chillies, cumin, garlic, oil and caraway seeds. It is available from supermarkets and Middle Eastern grocery stores.

turkey steaks with cranberry and hazelnut salad

¾ cup (150g) quinoa
¼ cup (75g) jellied cranberry sauce
1 tablespoon wholegrain mustard
6 turkey breast steaks (525g)
60g (2 ounces) baby spinach leaves
½ cup (65g) dried cranberries, chopped coarsely
½ cup (70g) roasted hazelnuts, chopped coarsely
½ cup loosely packed fresh mint leaves, torn
2 tablespoons lemon juice
1 tablespoon olive oil

1 Place quinoa in medium bowl; cover with boiling water. Stand 10 minutes; drain. Squeeze out as much excess water as possible.
2 Meanwhile, combine sauce, mustard and turkey in medium bowl.
3 Cook turkey on heated oiled barbecue (or grill or grill pan).
4 Meanwhile, combine quinoa, spinach, cranberries, nuts, mint, juice and oil in large bowl; season. Serve salad with turkey.

prep + cook time 35 minutes **serves** 4
nutritional count per serving 22.3g total fat (2.6g saturated fat); 2215kJ (530 cal); 43.3g carbohydrate; 36.7g protein; 5.9g fibre

note Quinoa (keen-wa) is a grain and is available from most health-food stores; keep refrigerated, as it spoils easily. You can use burghul instead.

tandoori turkey with pineapple salsa

¼ cup (75g) tandoori paste
¼ cup (70g) yogurt
4 x 100g (3½ ounce) turkey breast steaks
4 medium potatoes (800g), unpeeled
1 tablespoon vegetable oil
1 teaspoon each brown mustard seeds and
  cumin seeds

PINEAPPLE SALSA
½ small pineapple (450g), sliced thickly
1 medium red capsicum (bell pepper) (200g),
  chopped coarsely
⅓ cup coarsely chopped fresh mint
1 tablespoon lime juice

1   Combine paste, yogurt and turkey in large bowl. Cover; refrigerate 3 hours or overnight.
2   Boil, steam or microwave whole potatoes until tender; drain, cool.
3   Meanwhile, make pineapple salsa.
4   Cut potatoes into 1cm (½ inch) thick slices; combine potatoes, oil and seeds in medium bowl, season. Cook on heated oiled barbecue flat plate until browned lightly.
5   Drain turkey; discard marinade. Cook turkey on heated oiled barbecue (or grill or grill pan).
6   Serve turkey with potatoes and salsa.

PINEAPPLE SALSA Cook pineapple on heated oiled barbecue (or grill or grill pan) until browned lightly; chop coarsely. Combine pineapple with remaining ingredients in medium bowl.

prep + cook time 50 minutes (+ refrigeration)
serves 4
nutritional count per serving 13.6g total fat (2.2g saturated fat); 1693kJ (405 cal); 35.9g carbohydrate; 29.6g protein; 7.5g fibre

tomato and chipotle chilli chicken kebabs

Heat 1 tablespoon olive oil in medium saucepan; cook ½ coarsely chopped medium brown onion until browned lightly. Add 1 dried chipotle chilli, 2 small chopped tomatoes and ¼ cup water to pan; simmer, uncovered, about 15 minutes, stirring occasionally, until chilli and tomatoes soften. Cool. Remove and discard stem from the chilli; blend chilli with tomato mixture until smooth. Meanwhile, cut 750g (1½ pounds) chicken breast fillets into cubes. Thread chicken onto 12 skewers; brush with a little olive oil, season. Cook skewers on heated oiled barbecue (or grill or grill pan). Brush chicken with half the chilli sauce during the last few minutes of cooking. Serve with remaining chilli sauce, lime wedges and ¼ cup coriander (cilantro) leaves.

prep + cook time 35 minutes **makes** 12
nutritional count per kebab 4.9g total fat (1.1g saturated fat); 363kJ (87 cal); 0.5g carbohydrate; 10.2g protein; 0.2g fibre

spiced chicken kebabs with mint yogurt

Blend or process 1 coarsely chopped medium brown onion, 10cm (4 inch) piece chopped fresh ginger, 4 quartered garlic cloves, 2 tablespoons tomato paste and 1 teaspoon each ground cumin, black pepper, turmeric and garam masala until smooth. Transfer to large bowl. Add ¼ cup finely chopped coriander (cilantro), 1kg (2 pounds) minced (ground) chicken, 1 egg white and 1 cup stale breadcrumbs; season, mix well. With damp hands, shape mixture into 8 sausages; thread onto 8 skewers. Place on baking (parchment) paper lined tray. Refrigerate 1 hour. Combine 2 cups yogurt, ½ cup finely chopped fresh mint, 3 crushed cloves garlic and 2 tablespoons olive oil in medium bowl, season; stand 30 minutes. Cook skewers on heated oiled barbecue (or grill or grill pan). Serve with lemon wedges and mint yogurt.

prep + cook time 40 minutes (+ refrigeration) **makes** 8
nutritional count per kebab 8.5g total fat (2.4g saturated fat); 726kJ (174 cal); 8.2g carbohydrate; 15.5g protein; 0.9g fibre

soy chicken kebabs with orange hoisin sauce

Cut 750g (1½ pounds) chicken breast fillets into cubes; combine in large bowl with 2 tablespoons each sesame oil, peanut oil and lemon juice, ½ cup japanese soy sauce, 2 crushed garlic cloves and 1 teaspoon chopped fresh rosemary. Cover, refrigerate 2 hours. Thread chicken onto 12 skewers, reserving marinade. Cook skewers on heated oiled barbecue (or grill or grill pan), basting occasionally with marinade. Meanwhile, combine ⅓ cup each hoisin sauce and orange juice, 1 tablespoon rice vinegar, 1 finely chopped green onion (scallion) and 2 teaspoons sesame oil in bowl; mix well. Serve skewers with dipping sauce.

prep + cook time 35 minutes (+ refrigeration)
makes 12
nutritional count per kebab 8.1g total fat (1.7g saturated fat); 532kJ (127 cal); 2.7g carbohydrate; 10.7g protein; 0.7g fibre

chilli coriander chicken kebabs with pesto

Dry-fry 1 teaspoon each coriander seeds, chilli flakes, cumin seeds, sea salt and 2 teaspoons black peppercorns until fragrant; crush in mortar and pestle. Cut 750g (1½ pounds) chicken breast fillets into cubes; combine in medium bowl with spice mix and 1 tablespoon cornflour (cornstarch). Thread chicken onto 12 skewers; cook on heated oiled barbecue (or grill or grill pan). Meanwhile, blend or process 1 cup firmly packed fresh coriander (cilantro) leaves, 2 quartered garlic cloves, ¼ cup roasted walnuts, 1 tablespoon finely grated parmesan cheese and 1 teaspoon lemon juice until combined. With motor operating, gradually add ⅓ cup olive oil in a thin steady stream; season to taste. Serve skewers with coriander pesto.

prep + cook time 40 minutes **makes** 12
nutritional count per kebab 8.7g total fat (1.6g saturated fat); 513kJ (123 cal); 0.7g carbohydrate; 10.5g protein; 0.3g fibre

steaks, chops & ribs

smoky steak with kumara chips

2 medium kumara (orange sweet potato) (800g),
  unpeeled, cut into long strips
4 beef T-bone steaks (striploin) (1.2kg)
2 tablespoons light brown sugar
2 teaspoons smoked paprika
1 tablespoon each malt vinegar and
  worcestershire sauce
2 tablespoons tomato sauce (ketchup)
250g rocket (arugula), trimmed

1 Boil, steam or microwave kumara until tender;
drain.
2 Meanwhile, combine steaks with sugar, paprika,
vinegar and sauces in shallow bowl.
3 Cook kumara on heated oiled barbecue (or grill
or grill pan) about 10 minutes or until golden brown.
4 Cook undrained steaks on heated oiled barbecue.
Serve steaks with kumara chips and rocket.

prep + cook time 30 minutes **serves** 4
nutritional count per serving 27.5g total fat
(11.2g saturated fat); 2424kJ (580 cal);
34.9g carbohydrate; 46.9g protein; 4g fibre

thai beef skewers

Cut 625g (1¼ pounds) beef rump steak into 2.5cm (1 inch) pieces. Combine steak in medium bowl with 1 small finely chopped fresh red thai (serrano) chilli, 1 tablespoon fish sauce, ¼ cup finely chopped fresh coriander (cilantro), 2 crushed garlic cloves, 4cm (1½ inch) piece grated fresh ginger, 1 teaspoon light brown sugar and 1 tablespoon lime juice. Thread steak onto 8 bamboo skewers; cook on heated oiled barbecue (or grill or grill pan).

prep + cook time 25 minutes **makes** 8
nutritional count per skewer 1g total fat (0.4g saturated fat); 113kJ (27 cal); 0.2g carbohydrate; 4.3g protein; 0g fibre

ginger pork sausages

Dry-fry 1 teaspoon fennel seeds in small frying pan until fragrant. Break 1 star anise into pieces; grind in mortar and pestle with fennel seeds. Combine 750g (1½ pounds) minced (ground) pork, 3 crushed garlic cloves, 6cm (2¼ inch) piece grated fresh ginger, 2 tablespoons japanese soy sauce and 2 teaspoons dark brown sugar in large bowl. Form pork mixture into 8 sausage shapes; cook sausages on heated oiled barbecue flat plate (or grill). Serve with grilled flat bread and a green salad, if you like.

prep + cook time 30 minutes **serves** 4
nutritional count per serving 3.4g total fat (1.3g saturated fat); 299kJ (71 cal); 0.5g carbohydrate; 10g protein; 0.1g fibre

mexican pork and vegetable skewers

Boil, steam or microwave 1 trimmed corn cob. Drain, cool. Cut corn into 8 slices, then halve. Cut ½ small red onion into 16 thin wedges, ½ medium red capsicum (bell pepper) into 8 pieces and 400g (13 ounces) pork scotch steaks into 3cm (1¼ inch) pieces. Combine steak with 2 teaspoons mexican chilli powder in large bowl. Thread steak, onion, capsicum and 2 pieces of corn onto 8 skewers. Cook skewers on heated oiled barbecue (or grill or grill pan).

prep + cook time 25 minutes **makes** 8
nutritional count per skewer 0.6g total fat
(0.2g saturated fat); 110kJ (26 cal);
1.7g carbohydrate; 3.2g protein; 0.5g fibre

pork saltimbocca kebabs

Cut 650g (1¼ pounds) pork fillets into 2.5cm (1 inch) pieces. Combine fillets and 2 tablespoons chopped fresh sage in medium bowl. Cut 8 slices prosciutto in half lengthways. Wrap half the fillets in prosciutto; thread plain fillets alternately with prosciutto-wrapped fillets onto 8 skewers. Cook skewers on heated oiled barbecue (or grill or grill pan).

prep + cook time 20 minutes **makes** 8
nutritional count per kebab 0.7g total fat
(0.2g saturated fat); 93kJ (22 cal);
0g carbohydrate; 4.1g protein; 0g fibre

grilled tandoori steak

500g (1 pound) beef skirt steak
1 tablespoon each tamarind concentrate,
 tandoori paste and red curry paste
¼ cup (90g) honey

1 Combine steak with tamarind, pastes and honey in shallow bowl. Cover, refrigerate 1 hour or overnight.
2 Cook steak on heated oiled barbecue (or grill or grill pan). Remove from barbecue; cover, stand 5 minutes before cutting into thick slices.
3 Serve steak with fruit chutney, if you like.

prep + cook time 20 minutes (+ refrigeration)
serves 4
nutritional count per serving 8.3g total fat (2.9g saturated fat); 1062kJ (254 cal); 18.9g carbohydrate; 26.5g protein; 0.6g fibre

peppered beef roast

2 teaspoons each paprika and
  ground black pepper
1 tablespoon cracked black pepper
1 teaspoon ground cardamom
1kg (2 pound) boneless beef rib-eye
  (scotch fillet) roast
¾ cup (180ml) japanese soy sauce
½ cup (125ml) cider vinegar
2 teaspoons tomato paste
1 clove garlic, crushed

1 Combine spices in small bowl; rub all over beef. Combine beef with remaining ingredients in shallow bowl. Cover; refrigerate 3 hours or overnight, turning occasionally.
2 Heat covered barbecue to 180°C/350°F. Place roast in disposable baking dish; brush with marinade. Cook, using indirect heat, about 1½ hours. Remove roast from barbecue; cover, stand 5 minutes before slicing.

prep + cook time 1 hour 45 minutes (+ refrigeration)
serves 4
nutritional count per serving 15.5g total fat (6.8g saturated fat); 1542kJ (369 cal); 1.6g carbohydrate; 53.7g protein; 0.2g fibre

serving suggestion Serve with a green salad or barbecued vegetables.

red wine and garlic beef ribs

2.5kg (5 pounds) slabs barbecue beef ribs
½ cup (125ml) dry red wine
¼ cup (60ml) worcestershire sauce
2 tablespoons wholegrain mustard
⅓ cup (95g) tomato paste
¼ cup (55g) firmly packed light brown sugar
3 cloves garlic, crushed
1 tablespoon fresh thyme leaves

OLIVE AND BASIL MASH
750g (1½ pounds) potatoes, chopped coarsely
40g (1½ ounces) butter
½ cup (125ml) pouring cream, heated
¼ cup (40g) finely chopped seeded black olives
1 tablespoon finely chopped fresh basil

1 Combine ribs with remaining ingredients in large non-metallic baking dish; season. Cover; refrigerate 3 hours or overnight.
2 Drain ribs; reserve marinade. Cook ribs on heated oiled covered barbecue (or grill or grill pan), turning occasionally, about 1 hour. Remove ribs from barbecue; cover, stand 5 minutes.
3 Meanwhile, make olive and basil mash.
4 Bring reserved marinade to the boil in small saucepan; boil, uncovered, about 3 minutes or until sauce is thickened slightly.
5 Cut ribs into pieces; serve with mash and sauce.

OLIVE AND BASIL MASH Boil, steam or microwave potatoes until tender; drain. Mash potatoes with butter and cream until smooth. Stir in olives and basil; season to taste.

prep + cook time 1 hour 20 minutes (+ refrigeration)
serves 4
nutritional count per serving 40.1g total fat (22g saturated fat); 3411kJ (816 cal); 43.8g carbohydrate; 63.5g protein; 4.4g fibre

pepper steaks with fennel remoulade and apple

4 x 300g (10 ounce) beef T-bone (striploin) steaks
1 tablespoon olive oil
2 teaspoons cracked black pepper
2 medium apples (300g), sliced thinly crossways

FENNEL REMOULADE
1 large fennel bulb (550g), grated coarsely
½ cup (150g) whole-egg mayonnaise
1 tablespoon finely chopped fresh flat-leaf parsley
1 tablespoon lemon juice
2 teaspoons dijon mustard
2 teaspoons rinsed, drained baby capers,
  chopped finely

1 Make fennel remoulade.
2 Brush steaks all over with oil; sprinkle with pepper.
Cook steaks on heated oiled barbecue (or grill
or grill pan). Remove from barbecue; cover, stand
5 minutes.
3 Cook apple on heated oiled barbecue (or grill
or grill pan) until browned lightly.
4 Serve steak with fennel remoulade and apple,
and a green salad, if you like.

FENNEL REMOULADE Combine ingredients in
medium bowl; season to taste.

prep + cook time 50 minutes serves 4
nutritional count per serving 43.4g total fat
(13.1g saturated fat); 2671kJ (639 cal);
17.8g carbohydrate; 43.7g protein; 3.7g fibre

rib-eye steaks with couscous salad

4 beef rib-eye (scotch fillet) steaks (600g)
⅓ cup (80ml) japanese soy sauce
2 tablespoons rice wine vinegar
1 tablespoon honey
2cm (¾ inch) piece fresh ginger (10g), grated
2 cloves garlic, crushed

COUSCOUS SALAD
1½ cups (375ml) water
1 tablespoon olive oil
1½ cups (300g) couscous
15g (½ ounce) butter
⅓ cup coarsely chopped fresh flat-leaf parsley
2 green onions (scallions), sliced finely
1 medium tomato (150g), chopped coarsely
60g (2 ounces) baby spinach leaves
2 teaspoons finely grated lemon rind

1 Combine steaks with remaining ingredients in shallow bowl; cover, stand 30 minutes or refrigerate 3 hours.
2 Make couscous salad.
3 Remove steaks from marinade; discard marinade. Cook steaks on heated oiled barbecue (or grill or grill pan). Remove steaks from barbecue; cover, stand 5 minutes.
4 Serve steaks with couscous salad.

COUSCOUS SALAD Bring the water and oil to the boil in medium saucepan; remove from heat. Stir in couscous, cover; stand 5 minutes or until liquid is absorbed, fluffing with fork occasionally. Add butter; fluff with fork. Stir in remaining ingredients; season to taste.

prep + cook time 20 minutes (+ standing) serves 4
nutritional count per serving 18g total fat
(6.9g saturated fat); 2512kJ (601 cal);
65g carbohydrate; 42.3g protein; 2.1g fibre

chilli barbecued beef ribs

1¼ cups (310ml) cider vinegar
1 tablespoon each vegetable oil and molasses
2 teaspoons sea salt
1 teaspoon chilli flakes
¼ teaspoon cayenne pepper
⅔ cup (160ml) water
1.5kg (3 pounds) slab barbecue beef ribs

1 Make marinade by whisking vinegar, oil, molasses, salt, chilli, cayenne and the water in large jug until combined. Reserve ½ cup marinade; combine remaining marinade with ribs in large shallow dish; cover, refrigerate 3 hours or overnight.

2 Heat covered barbecue to 180°C/350°F. Place ribs in disposable baking dish. Cook, using indirect heat, about 35 minutes. Brush with some of the reserved marinade; cook a further 15 minutes, brushing ribs with remaining marinade every 5 minutes.
3 Remove ribs from barbecue; cover, stand 5 minutes. Cut into individual ribs to serve.

prep + cook time 1 hour (+ refrigeration) **serves** 4
nutritional count per serving 15.1g total fat (5.1g saturated fat); 1267kJ (303 cal); 4.8g carbohydrate; 34.5g protein; 0.1g fibre

notes Molasses is available from health-food stores. Treacle can be used in place of molasses.

beef and reef with tarragon butter

90g (3 ounces) butter, softened
2 cloves garlic, crushed
1 tablespoon finely chopped fresh tarragon
2 teaspoons dijon mustard
12 uncooked medium king prawns (shrimp) (540g)
4 x 250g (8 ounce) beef rib-eye (scotch fillet)
 steaks, bone in
185g (6 ounces) asparagus, trimmed

1 Combine butter, garlic, tarragon and mustard in small bowl. Place butter mixture on a piece of plastic wrap; shape into log, wrap tightly. Freeze about 1 hour or until firm; remove 15 minutes before serving.
2 Shell and devein prawns, leaving tails intact.
3 Cook steaks on heated oiled barbecue (or grill or grill pan). Remove steaks from barbecue; cover, stand 5 minutes.
4 Cook prawns and asparagus on heated oiled barbecue (or grill or grill pan).
5 Serve beef with asparagus and prawns; top with slices of butter.

prep + cook time 35 minutes (+ freezing) **serves** 4
nutritional count per serving 32.2g total fat
(17.8g saturated fat); 2169kJ (519 cal);
0.8g carbohydrate; 56.8g protein; 0.8g fibre

beef ribs with maple and sherry glaze

2 tablespoons finely chopped fresh lemon grass
3 kaffir lime leaves, shredded finely
1 teaspoon sea salt
2cm (¾ inch) piece fresh ginger (10g), grated
2 cloves garlic, quartered
6 racks beef short ribs (900g)
¾ cup (180ml) sweet sherry
½ cup (110g) firmly packed dark brown sugar
½ cup (125ml) pure maple syrup
2 tablespoons sesame oil
1 tablespoon five-spice powder

1 Pound lemon grass, lime leaves, salt, ginger and garlic in mortar and pestle until fragrant.
2 Combine lemon grass mixture with remaining ingredients in large bowl. Cover, refrigerate 3 hours or overnight.
3 Remove ribs from marinade; transfer marinade to medium saucepan.
4 Cook ribs on heated oiled barbecue (or grill or grill pan); season to taste. Remove ribs from barbecue; cover, stand 5 minutes.
5 Meanwhile, bring marinade to the boil; reduce heat, simmer, uncovered, about 10 minutes or until thickened.
6 Serve ribs drizzled with marinade.

prep + cook time 30 minutes (+ refrigeration)
serves 6
nutritional count per serving 13.3g total fat (3.9g saturated fat); 1634kJ (391 cal); 39.9g carbohydrate; 22.5g protein; 0.2g fibre

Kaffir lime leaves, also known as bai magrood, look like two glossy dark green leaves joined end to end, forming a rounded hourglass shape. They're available from Asian food stores, greengrocers and some major supermarkets. A strip of fresh lime peel may be substituted for each kaffir lime leaf.

sesame beef with asian slaw

2 tablespoons sesame seeds, toasted
1 clove garlic, crushed
1 teaspoon white sugar
3cm (1¼ inch) piece fresh ginger (15g), grated
2 tablespoons japanese soy sauce
1 tablespoon sake
4 beef rib-eye (scotch fillet) steaks (750g)
3 green onions (scallions), sliced diagonally

ASIAN SLAW
½ small wombok (350g), shredded coarsely
1 large carrot (180g), peeled, sliced thinly in strips
½ small daikon (200g), peeled, sliced thinly in strips
2 green onions (scallions), sliced thinly
2 tablespoons sesame seeds, toasted
½ cup (100g) whole-egg mayonnaise
¼ teaspoon japanese mustard
1½ tablespoons rice vinegar
1 tablespoon sake
½ teaspoon sesame oil
2 teaspoons japanese soy sauce
1 teaspoon white sugar

1 Crush seeds in mortar and pestle; combine with garlic, sugar, ginger, sauce, sake and steaks in shallow dish; cover, refrigerate 30 minutes.
2 Place onions in iced water for 10 minutes to curl; drain.
3 Remove steaks from marinade. Cook on heated oiled barbecue (or grill or grill pan); remove from barbecue. Cover beef, stand 5 minutes before slicing thinly.
4 Make asian coleslaw.
5 Serve steak with coleslaw; top with onion curls.

ASIAN COLESLAW Combine wombok, carrot, daikon, onion and seeds in large bowl. Whisk mayonnaise, mustard, vinegar, sake, oil, sauce and sugar in jug. Combine coleslaw with dressing just before serving; toss well.

prep + cook time 45 minutes (+ refrigeration)
serves 4
nutritional count per serving 24.4g total fat (5.7g saturated fat); 1977kJ (473 cal); 12.8g carbohydrate; 44.6g protein; 4.9g fibre

Japanese mustard is a hot mustard available as a ready-to-use paste in tubes, or as a powder, from Asian food shops. Use wasabi if you can't find it.

orange and fennel veal chops

2 medium oranges (480g)
3 baby fennel bulbs (400g), trimmed,
  sliced thickly lengthways
4 x 200g (6½ ounce) veal loin chops
1 tablespoon roasted fennel seeds
2 tablespoons olive oil
1 small red onion (100g), sliced thinly
75g (2½ ounces) baby rocket leaves (arugula)

1   Finely grate 2 teaspoons rind from oranges.
Segment oranges over small bowl, reserving
1 tablespoon of the juice.
2   Cook fennel on heated oiled barbecue (or grill
or grill pan) until tender; cool.
3   Meanwhile, combine veal with rind, seeds and
half the oil in medium bowl; season. Cook veal on
heated oiled barbecue (or grill or grill pan). Remove
veal from barbecue; cover, stand 5 minutes.
4   Combine fennel, orange segments, reserved
juice, remaining oil, onion and rocket in large bowl;
season to taste. Serve veal with fennel salad.

prep + cook time 40 minutes **serves** 4
nutritional count per serving 13.2g total fat
(2.7g saturated fat); 1221kJ (292 cal);
10.3g carbohydrate; 30.9g protein; 3.9g fibre

rosemary and garlic veal cutlets

4 thick veal cutlets (800g)
2 cloves garlic, sliced
8 small sprigs fresh rosemary
¼ cup (60ml) lemon juice
2 tablespoons olive oil

1 Make small incisions in each cutlet; insert garlic and rosemary into incisions.
2 Combine juice and oil in large shallow bowl; add cutlets, turn to coat in mixture, season. Cover, refrigerate 1 hour.
3 Cook cutlets on heated oiled barbecue (or grill or grill pan).

prep + cook time 25 minutes (+ refrigeration)
serves 4
nutritional count per serving 13.5g total fat (2.8g saturated fat); 1007kJ (241 cal); 0.6g carbohydrate; 28.9g protein; 0.3g fibre

chermoulla spiced veal cutlets

1 cup (250ml) olive oil
¾ cup firmly packed fresh coriander (cilantro)
  leaves
¾ cup firmly packed fresh flat-leaf parsley leaves
2 tablespoons grated palm sugar
3 fresh long red chillies, chopped coarsely
2 tablespoons finely grated lemon rind
2 tablespoons lemon juice
2 tablespoons caraway seeds, toasted
1 teaspoon ground turmeric
3 cloves garlic, quartered
4 french-trimmed veal cutlets (500g)

1 To make chermoulla mixture, blend or process oil, herbs, sugar, chilli, rind, juice, seeds, turmeric and garlic to a paste. Season.
2 Combine half the chermoulla with cutlets in large bowl; cover, refrigerate 3 hours or overnight. Refrigerate remaining chermoulla.
3 Season cutlets; cook on heated oiled barbecue (or grill or grill pan). Remove from barbecue; cover, stand 5 minutes.
4 Serve cutlets with remaining chermoulla. Serve with couscous, if you like.

prep + cook time 25 minutes (+ refrigeration)
serves 4
nutritional count per serving 59.8g total fat (9.2g saturated fat); 2780kJ (665 cal); 7.6g carbohydrate; 25.2g protein; 1.7g fibre

cinnamon marmalade pork

2 tablespoons orange marmalade
2 tablespoons olive oil
¼ teaspoon ground cinnamon
4 x 125g (4 ounce) pork loin medallions
125g (4 ounces) green beans, trimmed
2 medium oranges (480g)
2 ruby red grapefruit (700g)
1 tablespoon white wine vinegar
3 cups loosely packed watercress sprigs, trimmed

1 Whisk marmalade, half the oil and the cinnamon in large bowl until smooth. Add pork; turn to coat in marmalade mixture.
2 Cook pork on heated oiled barbecue (or grill or grill pan). Remove pork from barbecue; cover, stand 5 minutes.

3 Meanwhile, boil, steam or microwave beans until tender; drain. Rinse under cold water; drain.
4 Segment oranges and grapefruit, separately, over small bowl; reserve 1 tablespoon orange juice.
5 Whisk reserved juice, remaining oil and vinegar in large bowl. Add orange and grapefruit segments, beans and watercress; toss gently.
6 Serve pork with salad.

prep + cook time 45 minutes **serves** 4
nutritional count per serving 12.6g total fat
(2.2g saturated fat); 1488kJ (356 cal);
22.5g carbohydrate; 34.2g protein; 6.7g fibre

note You need to buy a 350g bunch of watercress.

maple mustard pork cutlets with apple salad

1 tablespoon wholegrain mustard
1 tablespoon dijon mustard
2 tablespoons pure maple syrup
1 tablespoon lemon juice
4 pork cutlets (940g)

APPLE SALAD
¼ cup (75g) whole-egg mayonnaise
2 teaspoons dijon mustard
1 tablespoon lemon juice
1 small apple (130g), quartered, sliced thinly
1 baby cos (romaine) lettuce (180g), trimmed,
  leaves separated
1 stalk celery (150g), trimmed, sliced thinly
2 tablespoons coarsely chopped pecans, toasted

1 Combine mustards, syrup and juice in medium
bowl; add cutlets, turn to coat in mixture.
2 Cook cutlets on heated oiled barbecue (or grill
or grill pan).
3 Meanwhile, make apple salad. Serve cutlets
with salad.

APPLE SALAD Combine mayonnaise, mustard and
juice in medium bowl. Add apple, mix gently. Add
lettuce and celery; toss gently. Sprinkle with nuts,
season to taste.

prep + cook time 30 minutes serves 4
nutritional count per serving 16.3g total fat
(3.3g saturated fat); 1484kJ (355 cal);
18.3g carbohydrate; 32.5g protein; 2.7g fibre

vindaloo pork grill

4 medium potatoes (800g), quartered
⅓ cup (100g) vindaloo paste
1 cup (280g) yogurt
4 pork cutlets (940g)
2 tablespoons finely chopped fresh mint
1 tablespoon lime juice
1 lebanese cucumber (130g)
1 medium carrot (120g)

1 Boil, steam or microwave potatoes until tender; drain, cool.
2 Combine paste and ¼ cup of the yogurt in large bowl. Add cutlets and potato; turn to coat.
3 Cook cutlets and potato on heated oiled barbecue (or grill or grill pan). Remove from barbecue; cover, stand 5 minutes.
4 Meanwhile, combine remaining yogurt with mint and juice in small bowl.
5 Using vegetable peeler, peel cucumber and carrot lengthways into thin ribbons.
6 Serve cutlets and vegetables with mint yogurt, and naan bread, if you like.

prep + cook time 45 minutes **serves** 4
nutritional count per serving 16.3g total fat (4.2g saturated fat); 1877kJ (449 cal); 30.4g carbohydrate; 40g protein; 6.4g fibre

five-spice, honey and tamarind pork spare ribs

2kg (4 pounds) racks american-style pork spare ribs
⅔ cup (160ml) chinese cooking wine
⅓ cup (80ml) light soy sauce
⅓ cup (75g) firmly packed light brown sugar
2 tablespoons thick tamarind concentrate
2 tablespoons honey
1 tablespoon peanut oil
1 tablespoon five-spice powder
2 fresh small red thai (serrano) chillies,
  chopped finely
2 cloves garlic, crushed
2.5cm (1 inch) piece fresh ginger (10g), grated

NOODLE SALAD
125g (4 ounces) dried rice stick noodles
300g (10 ounces) baby pak choy, quartered
125g (4 ounces) baby corn, halved lengthways
1 medium red capsicum (bell pepper) (200g),
  sliced thickly
1 tablespoon peanut oil
1 tablespoon lime juice
1 cup loosely packed fresh coriander (cilantro)
  leaves

1 Combine ribs with remaining ingredients in large non-metallic baking dish. Cover; refrigerate 3 hours or overnight.
2 Drain ribs; reserve marinade. Cook ribs on heated oiled covered barbecue (or grill or grill pan), turning occasionally, about 25 minutes. Remove ribs from barbecue; cover, stand 5 minutes.
3 Meanwhile, make noodle salad.
4 Bring reserved marinade to the boil in small saucepan; boil, uncovered, about 3 minutes or until sauce thickens slightly. Add 2 teaspoons of the hot sauce to the noodle salad.
5 Cut ribs into pieces; serve with noodle salad and hot sauce.

NOODLE SALAD Place noodles in large heatproof bowl; cover with boiling water. Stand until tender; drain. Rinse under cold water; drain. Meanwhile, cook vegetables on heated oiled barbecue until browned lightly and tender. Combine noodles, vegetables, oil, juice and coriander in large bowl.

prep + cook time 1 hour (+ refrigeration) serves 4
nutritional count per serving 26.8g total fat
(8.2g saturated fat); 3102kJ (742 cal);
45.2g carbohydrate; 72.5g protein; 3.4g fibre

Baby pak choy is very similar to baby buk choy, only it has pale green stems, rather than white, and has a flatter, spoon-shaped leaf, whereas the leaves of baby buk choy have more crinkles in them. They are cooked in the same way and are interchangeable in recipes.

sticky lemon and chilli pork ribs

1.2kg (2½ pounds) pork belly ribs
2 tablespoons olive oil
1 tablespoon finely grated lemon rind
1 tablespoon finely chopped fresh oregano
1 tablespoon caster (superfine) sugar
1 teaspoon dried chilli flakes

WHITE BEAN PUREE
400g (13 ounces) canned white beans,
  rinsed, drained
2 tablespoons each lemon juice and hot water
1 clove garlic, crushed

HERB SALAD
1 cup loosely packed fresh flat-leaf parsley leaves
½ cup loosely packed fresh small basil leaves
⅓ cup loosely packed fresh oregano leaves
125g (4 ounces) grape tomatoes, halved
1 tablespoon lemon juice
2 teaspoons olive oil

1 Combine ribs with remaining ingredients in
large bowl; season. Cover; refrigerate 3 hours
or overnight.
2 Cook ribs on heated oiled barbecue (or grill
or grill pan) about 20 minutes. Remove ribs from
barbecue; cover, stand 5 minutes.
3 Make white bean puree; make herb salad.
4 Serve ribs with puree and salad.

WHITE BEAN PUREE Blend or process ingredients
until smooth; season to taste.

HERB SALAD Combine ingredients in medium
bowl; season to taste.

prep + cook time 50 minutes (+ refrigeration)
serves 4
nutritional count per serving 31g total fat
(9.2g saturated fat); 2646kJ (633 cal);
7.1g carbohydrate; 79.7g protein; 3g fibre

vietnamese pork steaks with noodle salad

4 x 155g (5 ounce) pork butterfly steaks
1 tablespoon peanut oil
10cm (4 inch) stick fresh lemon grass (20g),
  chopped finely
2 cloves garlic, crushed
125g (4 ounces) rice vermicelli noodles
1 lebanese cucumber (130g), seeded, sliced thinly
1 medium carrot (120g), grated coarsely
4 red radishes (140g), trimmed, grated coarsely
1 cup finely shredded iceberg lettuce
2 tablespoons finely shredded fresh mint

SWEET CHILLI DRESSING
½ cup (125ml) water
⅓ cup (75g) caster (superfine) sugar
2 tablespoons lemon juice
1 tablespoon fish sauce
2cm (¾ inch) piece fresh ginger (10g), grated
1 fresh long red chilli, chopped finely

1 Make sweet chilli dressing.
2 Combine steaks, oil, lemon grass and garlic
in medium shallow dish. Cook steaks on heated
oiled barbecue (or grill or grill pan). Remove from
barbecue; cover, stand 5 minutes.
3 Meanwhile, place noodles in large heatproof
bowl; cover with boiling water. Stand until tender;
drain. Rinse under cold water; drain.
4 Combine noodles, dressing and remaining
ingredients in large bowl.
5 Serve steaks with noodle salad.

SWEET CHILLI DRESSING Combine the water,
sugar and juice in small saucepan; stir over heat
until sugar dissolves. Bring to the boil; boil,
uncovered, about 10 minutes or until mixture is
thickened slightly. Remove from heat; stir in
remaining ingredients.

prep + cook time 40 minutes serves 4
nutritional count per serving 10.4g total fat
(2.9g saturated fat); 1496kJ (358 cal);
29g carbohydrate; 36.2g protein; 2.4g fibre

barbecued pork ribs

4 racks american-style pork spare ribs (2.3kg)
1½ cups (375ml) barbecue sauce
1 cup (250ml) tomato sauce (ketchup)
1 tablespoon olive oil
20g (¾ ounce) fresh lemon thyme sprigs
4 cloves garlic, crushed

1   Combine ribs with sauces, oil, thyme and garlic in large shallow dish. Cover, refrigerate 3 hours or overnight, turning occasionally.
2   Cook ribs on heated oiled barbecue (or grill or grill pan), brushing with marinade occasionally. Serve with a warm potato salad, if you like.

prep + cook time 25 minutes (+ refrigeration)
serves 8
nutritional count per serving 7.4g total fat (2.1g saturated fat); 1275kJ (305 cal); 31.5g carbohydrate; 28.4g protein; 1.5g fibre

note You need about one bunch of lemon thyme for this recipe. Bruise the thyme before adding it to the marinade by firmly squeezing the sprigs together. This imparts more flavour to the marinade.

pork ribs with sticky barbecue sauce

1.75kg (3½ pounds) american-style pork spare ribs
1 cup (250ml) tomato sauce (ketchup)
½ cup (110g) firmly packed light brown sugar
2 cloves garlic, crushed
2 tablespoons worcestershire sauce
1 tablespoon cider vinegar
2 teaspoons smoked paprika

1 Bring large saucepan of water to the boil. Reduce heat to medium. Simmer ribs, covered, about 40 minutes or until tender. Drain.
2 Combine remaining ingredients in medium bowl with ribs.

3 Cook ribs on heated oiled barbecue (or grill or grill pan) about 15 minutes, basting with remaining marinade every 5 minutes.
4 Cut ribs into serving-sized portions.

prep + cook time 45 minutes **serves** 4
nutritional count per serving 15g total fat
(5.7g saturated fat); 2307kﺞ (552 cal);
44.7g carbohydrate; 60.2g protein; 1.6g fibre

marmalade and soy pork ribs

½ cup (170g) orange marmalade
1½ cups (375ml) orange juice
¼ cup (60ml) lemon juice
½ cup (125ml) dark soy sauce
¼ cup (55g) light brown sugar
½ teaspoon cayenne pepper
1.5kg (3 pounds) pork belly, bone in

1   Combine marmalade, juices, sauce, sugar and pepper in medium saucepan; stir over heat until marinade is almost boiling. Cool 10 minutes.
2   Combine pork with marinade in large shallow dish; cover, refrigerate overnight.
3   Heat covered barbecue to 180°C/350°F. Transfer pork and marinade to disposable baking dish; cover with foil. Cook, using indirect heat, about 2 hours, basting occasionally. Remove foil, cook a further 15 minutes. Remove ribs from barbecue; cover, stand 5 minutes before cutting.
4   Transfer marinade to small saucepan; boil, uncovered, until thickened slightly. Serve sauce with sliced ribs.

prep + cook time 2 hours 35 minutes (+ refrigeration)
serves 4
nutritional count per serving 18.2g total fat (6.1g saturated fat); 2675kJ (640 cal); 49.6g carbohydrate; 70.2g protein; 0.6g fibre

tuscan pork chops

1 cup (150g) sun-dried tomatoes in oil
1 cup firmly packed fresh basil leaves
¼ cup (40g) seeded black olives
¾ cup (180ml) lemon-infused olive oil
2 cloves garlic, quartered
6 pork forequarter chops (1.2kg)

1   Drain tomatoes, reserving 2 tablespoons of oil.
2   To make marinade, blend or process tomatoes, basil, olives, lemon olive oil, reserved sun-dried tomato oil and garlic until combined.
3   Combine marinade and chops in large shallow dish; cover, refrigerate 3 hours or overnight.
4   Drain chops, discard marinade; cook chops on heated oiled barbecue (or grill or grill pan).

prep + cook time 35 minutes (+ refrigeration)
serves 6
nutritional count per serving 42g total fat (7.4g saturated fat); 2337kJ (559 cal); 10.2g carbohydrate; 33.8g protein; 4g fibre

lamb cutlets with pomegranate and pumpkin salad

400g (13 ounce) piece jap pumpkin, unpeeled, sliced thinly
1 tablespoon pomegranate molasses
2 teaspoons ground cumin
1 teaspoon hot paprika
2 tablespoons olive oil
12 french-trimmed lamb cutlets (600g)
75g (2½ ounces) baby spinach leaves
½ cup (125ml) pomegranate seeds
125g (4 ounces) firm fetta cheese
1 tablespoon lime juice

1 Cook pumpkin on heated oiled barbecue (or grill or grill pan) until tender; transfer to large bowl, cool.
2 Meanwhile, combine molasses, spices and half the oil in large shallow dish; season. Add cutlets, turn to coat. Cook cutlets on heated oiled barbecue (or grill or grill pan).
3 Add spinach, seeds, crumbled cheese, juice and remaining oil to pumpkin; toss gently, season to taste. Serve cutlets with salad.

prep + cook time 50 minutes serves 4
nutritional count per serving 23.8g total fat (9.6g saturated fat); 1584kJ (379 cal); 14.5g carbohydrate; 25.2g protein; 3.6g fibre

note Pomegranate molasses is thick and brown with a concentrated flavour. It possesses tart and fruity qualities similar to balsamic vinegar. Available from Middle Eastern food stores, specialty food shops and better delicatessens.

lamb cutlets with tomato and coriander salsa

1 teaspoon ground coriander
½ teaspoon ground cumin
2 cloves garlic, crushed
1 teaspoon olive oil
2 tablespoons finely grated lemon rind
¼ cup (60ml) lemon juice
12 french-trimmed lamb cutlets (600g)

TOMATO AND CORIANDER SALSA
2 small tomatoes (180g), chopped finely
1 small red onion (80g), chopped finely
1 clove garlic, crushed
1 tablespoon red wine vinegar
1 tablespoon finely chopped fresh coriander
  (cilantro)

1 Combine spices, garlic, oil, rind and juice
in small bowl; rub mixture over cutlets, stand
10 minutes.
2 Cook cutlets on heated oiled barbecue (or grill
or grill pan).
3 Meanwhile, make tomato and coriander salsa.
Serve cutlets topped with salsa.

TOMATO AND CORIANDER SALSA Combine
ingredients in small bowl; season to taste.

prep + cook time 25 minutes serves 4
nutritional count per serving 8.7g total fat
(3.6g saturated fat); 698kJ (167 cal);
2.7g carbohydrate; 17.9g protein; 1.4g fibre

sumac lamb with eggplant puree and fattoush

1 large pitta bread (80g), sliced thinly
1 large eggplant (500g)
8 lamb loin chops (800g)
2 tablespoons sumac
1 clove garlic, crushed
1 tablespoon lemon juice
1 medium green capsicum (bell pepper) (200g),
  sliced thinly
1 small red onion (100g), sliced thinly
4 red radishes (140g), trimmed, cut into matchsticks
1 large tomato (220g), seeded, sliced thinly
½ cup each coarsely chopped fresh mint and
  flat-leaf parsley
1 tablespoon olive oil
1 tablespoon lemon juice, extra

1 Preheat oven to 180°C/350°F.
2 Place bread, in single layer, on oven tray. Bake about 5 minutes or until crisp. Cool.
3 Meanwhile, cut stalk from eggplant; pierce all over with a fork. Cook whole eggplant on heated oiled barbecue (or grill or grill pan), turning occasionally, about 15 minutes or until skin blackens and eggplant is tender. Transfer to medium bowl.
4 Sprinkle chops all over with sumac; cook on heated oiled barbecue (or grill or grill pan).
5 When eggplant is cool enough to handle, peel away skin; chop flesh coarsely. Blend or process eggplant, garlic and juice until smooth; season.
6 Make fattoush by combining bread with remaining ingredients in large bowl; season to taste.
7 Serve lamb with puree and fattoush.

prep + cook time 50 minutes **serves** 4
nutritional count per serving 18.7g total fat (7g saturated fat); 1672kJ (400 cal); 17.8g carbohydrate; 36.9g protein; 5.8g fibre

lamb, cheese and spinach gözleme

300g (10 ounces) lamb leg steak
2 teaspoons ground cumin
¼ teaspoon hot paprika
2 cups (300g) plain (all-purpose) flour
½ teaspoon table salt
¾ cup (180ml) warm water
300g (10 ounces) spinach, trimmed
1 cup (240g) ricotta cheese
2 tablespoons lemon juice
1 clove garlic, crushed
1 tablespoon finely chopped fresh mint
1 tablespoon olive oil

1 Sprinkle steak with combined spices; cook on heated oiled barbecue (or grill or grill pan). Remove from barbecue; cover, stand 10 minutes, then slice thinly.
2 Meanwhile, combine flour and salt in medium bowl. Gradually stir in the water; mix to a soft dough. Knead dough on floured surface about 5 minutes or until smooth and elastic. Return to bowl; cover.
3 Boil, steam or microwave spinach until wilted; rinse under cold water, drain. Squeeze out excess water; shred spinach finely. Combine spinach, cheese, juice, garlic and mint in medium bowl; season to taste.
4 Divide dough in half; roll each piece on floured surface into 25cm x 35cm (10 inch x 14 inch) rectangle. Divide cheese mixture across centre of each rectangle; top with lamb. Fold top and bottom edges of dough over filling; tuck in ends to seal.
5 Cook gözleme, both sides, on heated oiled barbecue (or grill or grill pan), over low heat, brushing with the oil until browned and heated through. Stand 5 minutes.
6 Cut each gözleme into 3 slices; serve with a green salad and lemon wedges, if you like.

prep + cook time 1 hour 10 minutes **serves** 6
nutritional count per serving 12.7g total fat (5g saturated fat); 1476kJ (353 cal); 36.9g carbohydrate; 20.9g protein; 2.8g fibre

spiced lemon lamb

½ cup (100g) preserved lemon rind, chopped coarsely (see tips)
¼ cup loosely packed fresh oregano leaves
¼ cup loosely packed fresh marjoram leaves
⅓ cup (80ml) olive oil
1 tablespoon caraway seeds, toasted
2 cloves garlic, crushed
1 tablespoon ground cumin
2 teaspoons mild paprika
8 lamb loin chops (800g)

1 Combine rind, herbs, 1 tablespoon of the oil, seeds and garlic in large mortar and pestle. Pound to a coarse paste.
2 Combine paste with remaining ingredients in large bowl; cover, refrigerate 2 hours or overnight.

3 Cook lamb on heated oiled barbecue (or grill or grill pan); season. Serve with couscous and yogurt, if you like.

prep + cook time 25 minutes (+ refrigeration)
serves 8
nutritional count per serving 15.7g total fat (4.4g saturated fat); 878kJ (210 cal); 0.6g carbohydrate; 16g protein; 0.8g fibre

tips To use preserved lemons, remove and discard the pulp and squeeze the juice from the rind. Rinse the rind well, then use as required.
To toast caraway seeds, place in a small dry frying pan over medium-low heat. Stir 1 minute or until fragrant.

minted lamb steaks with vegetable patties

2 tablespoons mint jelly
2 teaspoons hot water
¾ cup (200g) yogurt
⅔ cup (100g) plain (all-purpose) flour
1 medium zucchini (120g), grated coarsely
2 baby beetroot (beets) (50g), trimmed, peeled,
  grated coarsely
1 small brown onion (80g), chopped finely
2 cloves garlic, crushed
½ cup (60g) frozen peas
1 egg, beaten lightly
4 x 125g (4 ounce) lamb leg steaks

1 Whisk half the mint jelly and the water in small bowl until smooth. Stir in yogurt; cover, refrigerate until required.
2 Combine flour, zucchini, beetroot, onion, garlic, peas and egg in large bowl; season. Shape mixture into 8 patties.
3 Cook patties, in batches, on heated oiled barbecue flat plate, flattening with a spatula, until browned both sides and cooked through. Transfer to tray; cover to keep warm.
4 Meanwhile, brush remaining mint jelly over lamb; cook on heated oiled barbecue (or grill or grill pan). Remove from barbecue; cover, stand 5 minutes.
5 Serve lamb with patties and mint yogurt, and a rocket salad, if you like.

prep + cook time 45 minutes **serves** 4
nutritional count per serving 13.4g total fat
(5g saturated fat); 1588kJ (380 cal);
27.3g carbohydrate; 35.5g protein; 3.2g fibre

chermoulla lamb riblets

½ cup each finely chopped fresh coriander
 (cilantro) and flat-leaf parsley
3 cloves garlic, crushed
1 fresh long red chilli, chopped finely
1 tablespoon finely grated lemon rind
2 teaspoons ground cumin
1 teaspoon ground coriander
½ teaspoon hot paprika
⅓ cup (80ml) olive oil
1.5kg (3 pounds) racks lamb riblets
¼ cup (60ml) lemon juice

WARM COUSCOUS SALAD
1 cup (200g) couscous
1 cup (250ml) boiling water
3 green onions (scallions), sliced thinly
125g (4 ounces) grape tomatoes, halved
2 tablespoons roasted slivered almonds

1   Combine herbs, garlic, chilli, rind, spices and oil in large bowl. Place half the herb mixture into medium jug; cover, refrigerate. Combine riblets with herb mixture in bowl; cover, refrigerate 3 hours or overnight.
2   Cook riblets on heated oiled barbecue (or grill or grill pan), brushing with herb mixture, about 25 minutes.
3   Meanwhile, make warm couscous salad.
4   Stir juice into reserved herb mixture. Cut riblets into pieces; serve with couscous and herb mixture.

WARM COUSCOUS SALAD Combine couscous and the water in medium heatproof bowl; cover, stand about 5 minutes or until water is absorbed, fluffing with fork occasionally. Stir in remaining ingredients; season to taste.

prep + cook time 50 minutes (+ refrigeration)
serves 4
nutritional count per serving 33.4g total fat (9g saturated fat); 2621kJ (627 cal); 40.2g carbohydrate; 39.6g protein; 2.3g fibre

note Lamb riblets are just small cuts from the rib area.

mint and marjoram lamb cutlets with skordalia

⅓ cup (80ml) thick mint sauce
1 tablespoon wholegrain mustard
1 clove garlic, crushed
2 teaspoons dried marjoram
12 french-trimmed lamb cutlets (600g)

SKORDALIA
1 medium potato (200g), quartered
2 cloves garlic, crushed
1 tablespoon lemon juice
1 tablespoon white wine vinegar
¼ cup (60ml) olive oil

1 Make skordalia.
2 Meanwhile, combine sauce, mustard, garlic and marjoram in large shallow dish; add cutlets, turn to coat in mixture.
3 Cook cutlets on heated oiled barbecue (or grill or grill pan).
4 Serve cutlets with skordalia, and a greek salad and lemon wedges, if you like.

SKORDALIA Boil, steam or microwave potato until tender; drain. Push potato through food mill or fine sieve into large bowl; cool 10 minutes. Stir in garlic, juice and vinegar. Place potato mixture in blender or food processor. With motor operating, gradually add oil in a thin, steady stream, blending only until skordalia thickens (do not overmix).

prep + cook time 45 minutes serves 4
nutritional count per serving 20.8g total fat
(5.3g saturated fat); 1283kJ (307 cal);
10.3g carbohydrate; 18.6g protein; 1.3g fibre

note If the skordalia is too thick for your liking, thin it with a little warm water; a tablespoon or two is usually enough.

minted lemony lamb steaks

Combine 750g (1½ pound) piece lamb backstrap or leg steak with 2 tablespoons finely grated lemon rind, ⅓ cup lemon juice and 1 crushed garlic clove in medium bowl. Finely chop ½ cup fresh mint leaves; combine with ingredients in bowl. Cover, refrigerate overnight. Cook lamb on heated oiled barbecue (or grill or grill pan) about 20 minutes. Cover lamb; stand 5 minutes before slicing thinly. Serve with a green salad, if you like.

prep + cook time 20 minutes (+ refrigeration)
serves 4
nutritional count per serving 16g total fat
(5.7g saturated fat); 1308kJ (313 cal);
1.1g carbohydrate; 40.2g protein; 0.8g fibre

lamb kebabs on rosemary skewers

Remove leaves from bottom two-thirds of 8 fresh rosemary stalks; chop leaves coarsely, reserve. Sharpen stalk ends to a point. Cut 750g (1½ pounds) lamb fillets into 3cm (1¼ inch) cubes; thread onto rosemary skewers. Combine 1½ tablespoons of the chopped rosemary, 3 crushed garlic cloves, 2 tablespoons olive oil, 2 teaspoons finely grated lemon rind and 1 tablespoon lemon juice in small bowl; brush kebabs with garlic mixture. Cook kebabs on heated oiled barbecue (or grill or grill pan), brushing frequently with remaining garlic mixture. Serve kebabs with a greek salad, if you like.

prep + cook time 35 minutes **serves** 4
nutritional count per serving 42.3g total fat
(14g saturated fat); 2625kJ (628 cal);
9.8g carbohydrate; 50.6g protein; 3.6g fibre

black bean and lamb kebabs

Cut 500g (1 pound) lamb leg steaks into 2.5cm (1 inch) pieces. Combine lamb, 2 teaspoons chilli and garlic paste, 1 tablespoon black bean sauce, 2 tablespoons japanese soy sauce and 1 teaspoon sesame oil in medium bowl. Cut 3 green onions (scallions) into 4cm (1½ inch) lengths. Thread steak and onion onto 8 bamboo skewers. Cook skewers on heated oiled barbecue (or grill or grill pan). Sprinkle with sesame seeds.

prep + cook time 25 minutes **makes** 8
nutritional count per kebab 1.6g total fat (0.5g saturated fat); 123kJ (29.5 cal); 0.2g carbohydrate; 3.5g protein; 0.1g fibre

herbed lamb kofta with fetta

Combine ½ cup each finely chopped fresh flat-leaf parsley and coriander (cilantro), 1 lightly beaten egg, 600g (1¼ pounds) minced (ground) lamb, 2 teaspoons ground coriander, 1 teaspoon each ground cumin and sweet paprika and ½ teaspoon ground allspice in large bowl; season. Stir in 100g (3½ ounces) crumbled fetta cheese. Shape mixture into 8 sausages; thread and press onto 8 skewers. Cook skewers on heated oiled barbecue (or grill or grill pan). Serve with lemon wedges, yogurt and pitta bread, if you like

prep + cook time 30 minutes **makes** 8
nutritional count per kofta 23.8g total fat (1.2g saturated fat); 167kJ (40 cal); 0g carbohydrate; 4.6g protein; 0.1g fibre

the big event

sesame crusted tuna with grape and lychee salad

½ cup white long-grain rice (100g)
½ cup white sesame seeds (75g), roasted
½ cup black sesame seeds (75g), roasted
1kg (2 pound) piece tuna loin, trimmed
¼ cup (60ml) honey mustard sauce

GRAPE AND LYCHEE SALAD
2 tablespoons lime juice
2 tablespoons olive oil
565g (1 pound) canned lychees, drained, halved
250g (8 ounces) seedless black grapes, halved
40g (1½ ounces) trimmed watercress sprigs
¾ cup loosely packed fresh mint leaves
2 fresh long red chillies, sliced thinly

1 Make grape and lychee salad.
2 Dry-fry rice in medium frying pan until toasted lightly.
3 Blend or process rice and white sesame seeds about 2 minutes or until powdery. Combine powder in small bowl with black sesame seeds.
4 Cook tuna on heated oiled barbecue (or grill or grill pan) about 8 minutes or until browned all over. Remove from barbecue; cover, stand 10 minutes.
5 Coat tuna with honey mustard sauce. Place tuna on tray; coat with sesame mixture.
6 Slice tuna; serve with salad.

GRAPE AND LYCHEE SALAD Combine juice and oil in large bowl; add remaining ingredients. Toss gently, season to taste.

prep + cook time 30 minutes serves 6
nutritional count per serving 30.1g total fat (6.5g saturated fat); 2504kJ (599 cal); 29.8g carbohydrate; 50.6g protein; 4.6g fibre

whole fish with garlic and ginger

¾ cup loosely packed fresh coriander (cilantro)
 leaves, chopped coarsely
2 tablespoons finely chopped fresh lemon grass
8cm (3 inch) piece fresh ginger (40g), chopped finely
5 cloves garlic, sliced thinly
4 fresh long red chillies, sliced thinly
3 kaffir lime leaves, shredded finely
60g (2 ounces) butter, melted
4 medium lemons (560g), sliced thinly
4 x 600g (1¼ pounds) whole white fish

1 Combine coriander, lemon grass, ginger, garlic, chilli and lime leaves in medium bowl; season.
2 For each fish, layer 2 sheets of foil that are double the length of the fish, on bench. Brush foil centres with half the butter; top with lemon slices.
3 Score fish both sides; place on lemon, brush with remaining butter, season. Top each fish with ginger mixture. Gather corners of foil together; twist to enclose fish securely.
4 Cook fish in covered barbecue, using indirect heat, about 35 minutes. Remove from barbecue; stand 5 minutes before serving.

prep + cook time 50 minutes **serves** 4
nutritional count per serving 19.8g total fat (10.4g saturated fat); 2015kJ (482 cal); 3.7g carbohydrate; 66.2g protein; 4.6g fibre

notes We used barramundi, but you can use any whole white fish.
A strip of fresh lime peel may be substituted for each kaffir lime leaf.

Kaffir lime leaves, also known as bai magrood, look like two glossy dark green leaves joined end to end, forming a rounded hourglass shape. They're available from Asian-food stores, greengrocers and some major supermarkets.

Ask the butcher to butterfly the turkey for you.

turkey with strawberry and cherry salad

¾ cup (180ml) chicken consommé
¾ cup (150g) couscous
4 medium tomatoes (600g), seeded, chopped finely
¾ cup coarsely chopped fresh flat-leaf parsley
2 cloves garlic, crushed
1 tablespoon finely grated lemon rind
3kg (6 pound) turkey, butterflied
20g (¾ ounce) butter, melted

STRAWBERRY AND CHERRY SALAD
500g (1 pound) rocket (arugula), trimmed
250g (8 ounces) strawberries, hulled, halved
250g (8 ounces) cherries, seeded
¼ cup (60ml) balsamic vinegar
2 tablespoons olive oil
2 tablespoons finely shredded fresh basil

1 Bring consommé to the boil in small saucepan. Add couscous; cover, stand about 5 minutes or until liquid is absorbed, fluffing with fork occasionally.
2 Combine couscous with tomato, parsley, garlic and rind in medium bowl; season to taste.
3 Carefully ease skin away from turkey breasts and thighs. Push couscous mixture evenly under skin; brush turkey with butter.
4 Place turkey, skin-side up, in deep disposable baking dish. Cook turkey in covered barbecue, using indirect heat, about 1¾ hours, basting occasionally with pan juices. Remove turkey from barbecue; cover turkey, stand 10 minutes.
5 Meanwhile, make strawberry and cherry salad. Serve turkey with salad.

STRAWBERRY AND CHERRY SALAD Combine ingredients in large bowl; toss gently.

prep + cook time 2 hours 15 minutes serves 8
nutritional count per serving 27.1g total fat (7.6g saturated fat); 2454kJ (587 cal); 19.7g carbohydrate; 64.1g protein; 2.8g fibre

notes You need 2 bunches of rocket for this recipe. Use a good quality chicken stock instead of the consommé, if you prefer.

portuguese chicken with fig salad

4 pieces (170g), bottled, roasted red capsicums
  (bell peppers) drained
½ cup loosely packed fresh coriander (cilantro)
  leaves
¼ cup (90g) honey
¼ cup (60ml) olive oil
1 tablespoon balsamic vinegar
1 tablespoon finely grated lemon rind
1 tablespoon lemon juice
4 whole dried long red chillies
4 x 500g (1 pound) chickens, butterflied

FIG SALAD
2 tablespoons white balsamic vinegar
2 tablespoons lemon-infused olive oil
60g (2 ounces) baby spinach leaves
4 large figs (320g), quartered
½ cup (40g) shaved parmesan cheese

1 Blend or process capsicum, coriander, honey,
oil, vinegar, rind, juice and chilli until smooth.
Combine capsicum mixture with chickens in large
bowl; cover, refrigerate 3 hours or overnight.
2 Season chickens; cook on heated oiled barbecue
(or grill or grill pan) about 20 minutes. Remove from
barbecue; cover chickens, stand 10 minutes.
3 Make fig salad. Cut chickens into serving-sized
pieces; serve with salad.

FIG SALAD Combine vinegar and oil in screw-top
jar; shake well, season. Combine with remaining
ingredients in large bowl; toss gently.

prep + cook time 40 minutes (+ refrigeration)
serves 4
nutritional count per serving 65.9g total fat
(17.6g saturated fat); 3854kJ (922 cal);
27.2g carbohydrate; 55.3g protein; 3.2g fibre

note Butterflied chickens are available from
specialist chicken and butcher shops.

herb crusted beef fillet with kipfler potatoes

1kg (2 pounds) kipfler potatoes
1kg beef eye fillet, trimmed
2 medium red onions (340g), cut into wedges
2 tablespoons olive oil
¾ cup (210g) horseradish cream
¾ cup each loosely packed flat-leaf parsley, dill
  and tarragon leaves, chopped finely

1 Boil, steam or microwave potatoes until almost tender; drain, then cut in half.
2 Meanwhile, cook beef on heated oiled covered barbecue (or grill or grill pan) about 15 minutes until browned all over and cooked as desired. Remove from barbecue; cover beef, stand 10 minutes.
3 Combine potatoes with onion and oil in medium bowl. Cook on heated barbecue about 5 minutes or until potatoes are browned and tender; season. Cover to keep warm.
4 Combine beef with horseradish cream and herbs in large bowl; season. Slice beef; serve with potato mixture.

prep + cook time 40 minutes **serves** 6
nutritional count per serving 18.1g total fat (6.6g saturated fat); 1914kJ (458 cal); 30.1g carbohydrate; 40.5g protein; 5g fibre

Ask the butcher to tie the pork for you.

char siu pork with broccolini

1kg (2 pound) pork neck (scotch fillet roast)
⅓ cup (120g) char siu sauce
¼ cup (60ml) dry sherry
2 tablespoons honey
1 teaspoon five-spice powder
500g (1 pound) broccolini, trimmed
¼ cup (60ml) oyster sauce
2 tablespoons sesame oil

1 Tie pork with kitchen string at 1cm (½ inch) intervals. Combine pork, char siu sauce, sherry, honey and five-spice in large bowl; cover, refrigerate 3 hours or overnight.
2 Cook pork on heated oiled barbecue (or grill or grill pan) until browned all over.
3 Place pork in deep disposable baking dish; cook in covered barbecue, using indirect heat, about 1 hour 20 minutes. Cover pork, stand 10 minutes before slicing thinly.
4 Meanwhile, boil, steam or microwave broccolini until tender; drain. Combine broccolini with oyster sauce and oil. Serve pork with broccolini.

prep + cook time 1 hour 50 minutes (+ refrigeration)
serves 6
nutritional count per serving 25.1g total fat (7.7g saturated fat); 1923kJ (460 cal); 18.4g carbohydrate; 35.8g protein; 5.5g fibre

pineapple glazed ham with pomegranate and fennel salad

1 cup (250ml) unsweetened pineapple juice
1 cup (220g) firmly packed light brown sugar
1 teaspoon ground allspice
750g (1½ pound) piece boneless ham
2 tablespoons lemon juice
2 tablespoons lemon-infused olive oil
3 baby fennel bulbs (390g), sliced finely
100g (3 ounces) baby rocket leaves (arugula)
1 medium pomegranate (320g)
100g (3½ ounces) fetta cheese

prep + cook time 40 minutes (+ refrigeration)
serves 6
nutritional count per serving 17.3g total fat
(6g saturated fat); 1860kJ (445 cal);
45.3g carbohydrate; 27.1g protein; 2.9g fibre

1 Combine juice, sugar and spice in small saucepan; bring to the boil. Reduce heat; simmer, uncovered, about 4 minutes or until glaze is reduced by half.
2 Cut ham into 1cm (½ inch) thick slices. Combine ham and glaze in large shallow dish. Cover, refrigerate 3 hours or overnight.
3 Remove ham from glaze, transfer glaze to small saucepan; bring to the boil, simmer, uncovered, until thick and syrupy.
4 Cook ham on heated oiled barbecue (or grill or grill pan) until browned both sides.
5 To make salad, combine juice and oil in large bowl; add fennel and rocket, toss gently. Remove seeds from pomegranate; top salad with seeds and crumbled cheese.
6 Serve salad with ham; drizzle with glaze.

To remove the seeds from a pomegranate, cut it in half crossways and hold cut-side down over a bowl. Hit the outside skin of the fruit sharply with a wooden spoon – as hard as you can – and the seeds should fall out. If they don't, dig them out with a teaspoon.

lamb racks with capsicum pesto, asparagus and corn

1½ cups drained char-grilled red capsicums
  (bell peppers) (300g)
¼ cup pine nuts (40g), roasted
¼ cup (60ml) olive oil
¼ cup coarsely chopped fresh basil leaves
1 fresh long red chilli, chopped coarsely
1 tablespoon grated palm sugar
4 x 6-cutlet french-trimmed lamb racks (1.5kg)
2 large corn cobs (800g), husked
500g (1 pound) asparagus, trimmed
3 shallots (75g), sliced thinly
2 tablespoons finely chopped fresh flat-leaf parsley
1 tablespoon lime juice
½ teaspoon chilli powder

1 Blend or process capsicum, nuts, oil, basil, chopped chilli and sugar until smooth; season. Combine half the paste with lamb racks in large shallow bowl; cover, refrigerate 3 hours or overnight.
2 Place lamb in deep disposable baking dish; cook in covered barbecue using indirect heat about 15 minutes. Cover lamb, stand 10 minutes before cutting into serving-sized portions.
3 Meanwhile, boil, steam or microwave corn until tender; drain. When cool enough to handle, cut corn kernels, in small slabs, from cobs.
4 Cook asparagus on heated oiled barbecue (or grill or grill pan) until tender. Combine shallots, parsley, juice and powdered chilli in small bowl; drizzle over asparagus and corn.
5 Serve lamb with corn, asparagus and reserved paste thinned with a little hot water, if necessary.

prep + cook time 45 minutes (+ refrigeration)
serves 8
nutritional count per serving 17.8g total fat
(4.1g saturated fat); 1359kJ (325 cal);
16.7g carbohydrate; 22g protein; 5.3g fibre

Almond paste, also known as almond butter or spread, is available from health-food stores or the health-food section of larger supermarkets.

almond mustard pork with nashi and orange slaw

¾ cup (160g) almond paste
2 tablespoons wholegrain mustard
2 tablespoons honey
2 tablespoons peanut oil
1 teaspoon ground nutmeg
4 pork fillets (960g)

NASHI AND ORANGE SLAW
2 large oranges (850g)
2 medium nashi (400g)
4 small red radishes (140g)
2 cups finely shredded wombok (80g)
½ cup loosely packed fresh mint leaves,
  shredded finely
2 tablespoons avocado oil

1 Make nashi and orange slaw.
2 Combine paste, mustard, honey, oil and nutmeg in large bowl; add pork, turn to coat in mixture. Cover, refrigerate 3 hours or overnight.
3 Cook pork on heated oiled barbecue (or grill or grill pan) about 10 minutes or until browned all over, brushing occasionally with marinade. Cover; stand pork 10 minutes before slicing thickly.
4 Serve pork with slaw.

NASHI AND ORANGE SLAW Segment oranges over large bowl, reserving 2 tablespoons of the juice. Cut nashi and radishes lengthways into thin slices, cut slices into matchstick-sized pieces. Combine nashi and radish with orange and juice in bowl; add remaining ingredients, toss to combine. Season to taste.

prep + cook time 35 minutes (+ refrigeration)
serves 8
nutritional count per serving 20.5g total fat (2.9g saturated fat); 1613kJ (386 cal); 18g carbohydrate; 30.8g protein; 4.4g fibre

note If you can't find avocado oil, use olive oil.

spiced butterflied lamb with date and pistachio couscous

1½ cups (420g) yogurt
2 tablespoons mustard seed oil
2 fresh long red chillies, chopped coarsely
3 cloves garlic, quartered
2cm (¾ inch) piece fresh ginger (10g), grated finely
1 teaspoon each ground cumin, coriander, cardamom and cinnamon
2kg (4 pound) lamb leg, butterflied

DATE AND PISTACHIO COUSCOUS
2 cups (500ml) chicken consommé
2 cups (400g) couscous
2 tablespoons olive oil
½ cup fresh dates (125g), seeded, chopped coarsely
½ cup (70g) pistachios, roasted, chopped coarsely
1 tablespoon finely grated lemon rind
2 tablespoons fresh lemon juice
2 tablespoons coarsely chopped fresh flat-leaf parsley

1 Blend or process yogurt, oil, chilli, garlic, ginger and spices until smooth. Combine yogurt mixture in large shallow dish with lamb; cover, refrigerate 2 hours or overnight.
2 Place lamb in deep disposable baking dish; cook in covered barbecue, using indirect heat, about 45 minutes. Remove from barbecue; cover with foil, stand 15 minutes.
3 Meanwhile, make date and pistachio couscous.
4 Slice lamb; serve with couscous.

DATE AND PISTACHIO COUSCOUS Bring consommé to the boil in medium saucepan; remove from heat, add couscous. Cover; stand couscous about 5 minutes or until liquid is absorbed, fluffing with fork occasionally. Stir in remaining ingredients; season to taste.

prep + cook time 1 hour 15 minutes (+ refrigeration)
serves 8
nutritional count per serving 29g total fat (9.7g saturated fat); 2855kJ (683 cal); 51.2g carbohydrate; 52.7g protein; 2.6g fibre

note If you can't find fresh dates, use ½ cup (70g) coarsely chopped seeded dried dates.

glossary

BALSAMIC GLAZE rich, dark brown glaze made from concentrated balsamic vinegar; used to glaze, or to enrich a sauce for game or duck.

BEANS, WHITE in this book, some recipes may call for 'white beans', a generic term we use for cannellini, haricot, navy or great northern beans, all of which can be substituted for each other.

BREADCRUMBS
packaged fine-textured, crunchy, purchased white breadcrumbs.
stale one- or two-day-old bread made into crumbs by blending or processing.

BURGHUL made from whole wheat kernels, which are steamed, dried and toasted before cracking into several sizes so they develop a rich, nutty flavour. Because it is already partially cooked, burghul only requires minimal cooking. Cracked wheat, on the other hand, is raw whole wheat.

BUTTER use salted or unsalted (sweet) butter; 125g is equal to one stick (4 ounces) of butter.

CAJUN SEASONING used to give an authentic USA deep-south spicy cajun flavour to food. A blend of assorted herbs and spices that can include paprika, basil, onion, fennel, thyme, cayenne and tarragon.

CAYENNE PEPPER see chilli.

CHEESE, HALOUMI a firm, cream-coloured sheep-milk cheese matured in brine; tastes somewhat like a minty, salty fetta in flavour. Haloumi can be grilled or fried, briefly, without breaking down. Should be eaten while still warm as it becomes tough and rubbery on cooling.

CHICKEN
breast fillet we use single breast fillets, halved, skinned and boned.
drumette small fleshy part of the wing between shoulder and elbow, trimmed to resemble a small drumstick.
drumstick leg with skin intact.
small chickens (also known as poussin or spatchcock); no more than 6 weeks old, weighing a maximum 500g (1 lb).

CHILLI available in many different types and sizes. Use rubber gloves when seeding and chopping fresh chillies as they can burn your skin. Removing seeds and membranes lessens the heat level.
cayenne pepper a long, thin-fleshed, extremely hot red chilli usually sold dried and ground.
chipotle are what fresh jalapeño chillies are called after they've been dried and smoked; have a deep, intensely smoky flavour rather than a searing heat. Dark brown, almost black in appearance, they're available from specialty spice stores and gourmet delicatessens.
flakes deep-red, dehydrated chilli slices and whole seeds.
long red available fresh and dried; a term used for any moderately hot, long (about 6cm-8cm), thin chilli.
mexican chilli powder a spicy blend of chilli, cumin seeds, paprika, garlic, oregano and pepper; it has a mild/medium heat level.
powder the Asian variety, made from dried, ground thai chillies, is the hottest; can be used as a substitute for fresh chillies in the proportion of ½ teaspoon ground chilli powder to 1 medium chopped fresh chilli.

CHINESE COOKING WINE also known as shao hsing or chinese rice wine; made from fermented rice, wheat, sugar and salt with a 13.5 per cent alcohol content. Can be found in Asian food shops; if you can't find it, replace with mirin or sherry.

CORIANDER (cilantro) both the stems and the roots of coriander are used in cooking; wash well before using. Also available ground or as seeds; these should not be substituted for fresh coriander as the tastes are completely different.

CUMIN also known as zeera or comino; a spice with a nutty flavour. Available in seed or ground form.

CORNFLOUR also known as cornstarch; used as a thickening agent. Available as 100% maize (corn) and wheaten cornflour.

COUSCOUS a fine, grain-like cereal product made from semolina dough, sieved then dehydrated to produce minuscule even-sized pellets of couscous; is rehydrated by steaming, or with the addition of a warm liquid, and swells to three or four times its original size.

CREAM we use fresh cream, also known as pouring cream and pure cream, unless otherwise stated.

DIJONNAISE mayonnaise combined with dijon mustard.

DUKKAH an Egyptian spice blend made of roasted nuts and a mix of aromatic spices. It is available from Middle Eastern food stores, specialty spice stores and some supermarkets.

EGGPLANT a purple-skinned vegetable also known as aubergine.
baby also known as finger or japanese eggplant; very small and slender. Tender with a sweet taste.

FIVE-SPICE POWDER also known as chinese five-spice; a fragrant mixture of ground cinnamon, star anise, cloves, sichuan pepper and fennel seeds.

FLOUR, PLAIN an all-purpose flour made from wheat.

GARAM MASALA a blend of spices including cardamom, cinnamon, cloves, coriander, fennel and cumin, roasted and ground together. Black pepper and chilli can be added for a hotter version.

HORSERADISH CREAM a creamy prepared paste of grated horseradish, vinegar, oil and sugar.

KECAP MANIS see sauces.

KUMARA see sweet potato.

MAPLE SYRUP, PURE a thin syrup distilled from the sap of the maple tree. Maple-flavoured syrup or pancake syrup is not an adequate substitute for the real thing.

MINCE also known as ground meat.

MINT JELLY a very thick sauce made from mint leaves, sugar, lemon juice and pectin.

MIXED SALAD LEAVES mixed baby leaves also sold as salad mix, mesclun or gourmet salad mix; a mixture of assorted young lettuce and other green leaves.

MOLASSES a very thick, brown to deep black, honey-like syrup made from processed sugar cane or beet sugar. Has a slightly bitter flavour.

MUSTARD
dijon a pale brown, fairly mild French mustard.
japanese a hot mustard available in ready-to-use paste in tubes or powder from Asian food shops.
powder finely ground white (yellow) mustard seeds.
seeds available as white (also known as yellow seeds) and brown (also known as black seeds). Store seeds for up to a year in a dry, dark place.
wholegrain also known as seeded mustard. This French-style coarse-grain mustard is made from crushed mustard seeds combined with a dijon-style mustard.

NASHI a member of the pear family but resembling an apple with its pale-yellow-green, tennis-ball-sized appearance; more commonly known as the Asian pear. Is crisp, juicy and ready to eat as soon as it is picked, and has a distinctive texture and mildly sweet taste.

NOODLES
dried rice stick only differ from rice vermicelli in that they are thicker. The two can be interchanged.
rice vermicelli (dried rice noodles) a thin noodle also known as sen mee, mei fun or bee hoon. Used throughout Asia in spring rolls and cold salads; made with rice flour.

OIL
avocado pressed from the flesh of the avocado fruit. Can handle high heat without burning. It is high in monounsaturated fats and vitamin E.
macadamia extracted from crushed macadamias; has a high level of monounsaturated fats, and a high smoke point. Has a nutty flavour and aroma.

mustard cold-pressed oil is pressed from the whole seed, with no heat treatment, and is then filtered and bottled. Is rich and full-bodied with a buttery, nutty flavour, but without the heat or strong mustard taste. It has a low saturated fat content and is high in monounsaturated and omega-3 fats.
olive made from ripened olives. Extra virgin and virgin are the best, while extra light or light refers to taste not fat levels. *Lemon-infused olive oil* is available from some major supermarkets and delicatessens. To make your own, add a few strips of thin lemon rind to the measured olive oil, and stand for a few hours so the lemon flavour develops.
peanut pressed from ground peanuts; most commonly used oil in Asian cooking because of its high smoke point (capacity to handle high heat without burning).
sesame made from roasted, crushed, white sesame seeds; a flavouring rather than a cooking medium.
vegetable sourced from plants rather than animal fats.

PARSLEY, FLAT-LEAF also known as continental or italian parsley.

PEPPERCORNS
black the most common peppercorn; picked when the berry is not quite ripe, then dried until it shrivels and the skin turns dark brown to black. Strong-flavoured and slightly hot with a hint of sweetness.
sichuan also known as szechuan or chinese pepper. A mildly hot spice that comes from the prickly ash tree. Although it is not related to the peppercorn family, its small, red-brown aromatic sichuan berries look like black peppercorns, and they have a distinctive peppery-lemon flavour and aroma.

PERI PERI (piri piri) available as a powder or sauce; made from a blend of chillies, this hot chilli paste is typically used in the foods of South Africa and parts of India. Available from major supermarkets, spice shops and some delicatessens.

POMEGRANATE MOLASSES thicker, browner and more concentrated in flavour than grenadine, the sweet, red pomegranate syrup used in cocktails. Has a tart, fruity quality. Available at Middle Eastern food stores, specialty food shops and better delicatessens.

QUAILS small, delicately flavoured, domestically grown game birds ranging in weight from 250g to 300g (8oz-10oz); also known as partridge.

POPPY SEEDS tiny black seeds with a pungent flavour; store in an airtight container in a cool place or freezer.

SAKE Japan's favourite rice wine; used in cooking, marinating and as part of dipping sauces. If sake is unavailable, dry sherry, vermouth or brandy can be used as a substitute.

SAMBAL OELEK (also ulek or olek) Indonesian in origin, this salty paste is made from ground chillies, ginger, garlic and vinegar.

SAUCES
barbecue a spicy, tomato-based sauce used to marinate or baste, or as a condiment.
black bean a Chinese sauce made from fermented soya beans, spices, water and flour.
char siu a Chinese barbecue sauce made from sugar, water, fermented soya bean paste, honey, soy sauce, malt syrup and spices. It can be found at most supermarkets.
cranberry made of cranberries cooked in sugar syrup.
fish also called nam pla or nuoc nam; made from pulverised salted, fermented fish, most often anchovies. Has a pungent smell and strong taste; use sparingly.
hoisin a thick, sweet and spicy sauce; made from salted, fermented soya beans, onions and garlic.
mint made from finely chopped mint leaves soaked in vinegar and a small amount of sugar.
oyster Asian in origin; a rich, brown sauce made from oysters and their brine, cooked with salt and soy sauce, and thickened with starches.

soy made from fermented soya beans. Several variations are available in most supermarkets and Asian food stores.

dark soy deep brown, almost black in colour; rich, with a thicker consistency than other types. Pungent but not particularly salty, it is good for marinating.

japanese soy an all-purpose, low-sodium soy sauce made with more wheat content than its Chinese counterparts; fermented in barrels and aged. Possibly the best table soy and the one to choose if you only want one variety.

kecap manis a dark, thick, sweet soy sauce, sweetened by either molasses or palm sugar when brewed.

light soy a fairly thin, pale but salty-tasting sauce; used in dishes in which the natural colour of the ingredients is to be maintained. Not to be confused with salt-reduced or low-sodium soy sauces.

sweet chilli a comparatively mild, Thai-style sauce made from red chillies, sugar, garlic and vinegar.

Tabasco brand name of an extremely fiery sauce made from vinegar, thai red chillies and salt.

tomato also known as ketchup or catsup; a flavoured condiment made from tomatoes, vinegar and spices.

worcestershire a dark-coloured condiment made from soy sauce, garlic, tamarind, onions, molasses, lime, anchovies, vinegar and various other seasonings.

SEAFOOD

firm white fish fillets blue-eye, bream, flathead, swordfish, ling, whiting, jewfish or snapper are all good choices. Check for any small pieces of bone in the fillets and use tweezers to remove them.

garfish small, long and slender with a readily distinguished beak-like elongation of the lower jaw. The flesh is sweet with a firm texture, but watch out for the fine bones. Large sardines or whiting can be substituted for garfish

prawns also known as shrimp.

SUGAR

brown, light an extremely soft, finely granulated sugar retaining molasses for its characteristic colour and flavour.

Dark brown sugar is a moist sugar with a rich distinctive full flavour coming from molasses (it has more molasses than light brown sugar).

caster also known as superfine or finely granulated table sugar.

white a coarsely granulated table sugar, also known as crystal sugar.

SUMAC a purple-red, astringent spice ground from berries growing on shrubs that flourish wild around the Mediterranean; adds a tart, lemony flavour to foods.

SWEET POTATO

kumara Polynesian name of an orange-fleshed sweet potato often confused with yam. It has a musky, sweet flavour and caramelises well when baked.

purple beneath its purple skin lies a white flesh, which discolours quickly when cut. When peeled and cut, place pieces into water to stop this from happening.

white the opposite of purple sweet potato – beneath its white skin lies a purple-coloured flesh. It is less sweet than the others and has an earthy flavour. It is best roasted.

TAHINI sesame seed paste available from Middle Eastern food stores and most supermarkets.

TAMARIND CONCENTRATE the commercial distillation of tamarind pulp into a condensed paste. Used straight from the container, with no soaking or straining required; can be diluted with water according to taste. Found in Asian food stores and supermarkets.

TOMATOES

paste triple-concentrated tomato puree used to flavour soups, stews, sauces and casseroles.

semi-dried partially dried tomato pieces in olive oil; softer and juicier than sun-dried, these are not a preserve, so they do not keep as long as sun-dried tomatoes.

sun-dried we use sun-dried tomatoes packaged in oil, unless otherwise specified.

truss small vine-ripened tomatoes with vine still attached.

VINE LEAVES (grape vine leaves/grapevine leaves) come cryovac-packed or packed in jars in brine, and can be found in most Middle Eastern food stores, delicatessens and major supermarkets.

VINEGAR

balsamic made from the juice of Trebbiano grapes; it is a deep rich brown colour with a sweet and sour flavour. There are many balsamic vinegars now on the market, varying in pungency and quality depending on how long they have been aged. Quality can be determined up to a point by price; use the most expensive sparingly.

balsamic white condiment is a clear, lighter version of balsamic vinegar; it has a fresh, sweet, clean taste.

brown malt made from fermented malt and beech shavings.

cider (apple cider) made from fermented apples.

red wine based on fermented red wine.

rice a colourless vinegar made from fermented rice and flavoured with sugar and salt. Also known as seasoned rice vinegar.

rice wine made from rice wine lees (sediment left after fermentation), salt and alcohol.

sherry made from a blend of wines left in wood vats to mature, where they develop a rich, mellow flavour.

white wine made from a blend of white wines.

WASABI PASTE an Asian horseradish sold as a powder or paste.

ZUCCHINI also known as courgette; small, pale- or dark-green, yellow or white vegetable belonging to the squash family. Harvested young, its edible flowers can be stuffed, then deep-fried or oven-baked to make a delicious appetiser.